SOCIAL
SECURITY
THE PHONY CRISIS

SOCIAL SECURITY
THE PHONY CRISIS

Dean Baker
and
Mark Weisbrot

THE UNIVERSITY OF CHICAGO PRESS

Chicago and London

Dean Baker is a senior research fellow at the Century Foundation in New York City and the Preamble Center in Washington, D.C., and a research associate at the Economic Policy Institute. He received his Ph.D in Economics from the University of Michigan. He writes the Economic Reporting Review (available at www.fair.org), a weekly on-line commentary on media coverage of economic issues, and his recent book, *Getting Prices Right: The Debate Over the Consumer Price Index*, won the *Choice* award for one of the best economic books of 1998.

Mark Weisbrot is research director at the Preamble Center and a research associate at the Economic Policy Institute. He received his Ph.D in Economics from the University of Michigan. His weekly column is distributed by Knight-Ridder/Tribune Media Services, and his opinion pieces have appeared in the *Los Angeles Times*, the *Washington Post*, and the *Boston Globe*.

The University of Chicago Press, Chicago 60637
The University of Chicago Press, Ltd., London
© 1999 by The University of Chicago
All rights reserved. Published 1999

08 07 06 05 04 03 01 00   3 4 5
ISBN: 0-226-03544-1 (cloth)

Library of Congress Cataloging-in-Publication Data

Baker, Dean, 1958–
    Social security : the phony crisis / Dean Baker and Mark Weisbrot.
        p.   cm.
    Includes bibliographical references and index.
    ISBN 0-226-03544-1 (alk. paper)
    1. Social security—United States—Finance.   I. Weisbrot, Mark.
II. Title.
HD7125.B2785   1999   99-28058
368.4'301'0973—dc21   CIP

♾ The paper used in this publication meets the minimum requirements of the American National Standard for Information Sciences — Permanence of Paper for Printed Library Materials, ANSI Z39.48.1992.

Dedication

To the thousands of activists, including many senior citizens, who have generously volunteered their time and energy to defending Social Security for future generations against an avalanche of misinformation, disinformation, and powerful political and financial interests. They will win.

Contents

Preface

THE ONLY REASON TO CARE about economic policy is because it can be used to improve people's lives. Few policies have made as much difference in this regard as Social Security. It has allowed tens of millions of workers to enjoy a decent retirement over the last six decades, and it provides insurance against disability and early death. Social Security creates an element of security in an economic environment that fosters insecurity. For this reason, it deserves the enormous public support that it has consistently registered.

The Social Security system is currently threatened more than ever before in its 64-year history. The problem is not financial, economic, or demographic—the standard projections provide no basis for serious concern about the program's financial survival. Nor is the problem a lack of political support for Social Security. This continues to be overwhelming. The problem is that people have become convinced that the program is in serious trouble. As a result of a steady stream of misinformation, the public could possibly allow a program that it values immensely to be seriously undermined or dismantled. Ironically, the greatest threat to Social Security has come from its would-be rescuers.

This book is written in the hope that the truth can make a difference. We believe that if people understand the basic facts surrounding the Social Security program, most of which are not in dispute, they will not tolerate its destruction. Some readers may reach different conclusions than we do about the merits of the current system, but it would be a tragedy if misinformation determined the outcome of the national debate.

Acknowledgments

MANY PEOPLE READ and commented on all or part of this manuscript or earlier work from which it is derived. They include Eileen Appelbaum, Patricia Bauman, Jared Bernstein, Gary Burtless, Robert Haveman, Helene Jorgensen, Richard Leone, Robert Naiman, Joseph Quinn, Max Sawicky, John Schmitt, Joe White, and Howard Young. Special thanks are in order to Tammy Lyn Donohue, Joyce Kim, and Jon Schwarz, whose help with research was invaluable. The late Robert Eisner was tremendously helpful in developing many of the arguments presented here. He will be missed.

Introduction

WE HAVE A CHANCE, said President Clinton, to "fix the roof while the sun is still shining." He was talking about dealing with Social Security immediately, while the economy is growing and the federal budget is balanced. The audience was a regional conference on Social Security, in Kansas City, Missouri, that the White House had helped bring together.

The roof analogy is illuminating, but we can make it more accurate. Imagine that it's not going to rain for more than 30 years. And the rain, when it does arrive (and it might not), will be pretty light. And imagine that the average household will have a lot more income for roof repair by the time the rain approaches.

Now add this: most of the people who say they want to fix the roof actually want to knock holes in it.

This is the situation facing Social Security, and it is well known to those who have looked at the numbers. The program will take in enough revenue to keep all of its promises for over 30 years, without any changes at all. Thirty years is a long time—it's hard to think of any other program that can claim to be secure for that long. Furthermore, the forecast of a shortfall in 2034 is based on the economy limping along at less than a 1.7 percent annual rate of growth—about half the rate of the previous three decades.[1] If the economy were to grow at 1998's rate, for example, the system would never run short of money.

---

1. All numbers in this book pertaining to Social Security's projected or current finances are, unless otherwise noted, taken from the 1999 *Annual Report of the Board of Trustees of the Federal Old-Age and Survivors Insurance and Disability Insurance Trust Funds*, published by the Social Security Administration.

But even if the dismal growth forecasts turn out to be true, and the program eventually runs a deficit, it's not exactly the end of the world. For one thing, the Social Security system would be far from "broke." While it would indeed be short of revenue to maintain promised benefits, it would still be able to pay retirees higher real benefits than they are receiving today. And the nation has managed obligations of this size in the past: the financing gap would be roughly equal to the amount by which we increased military spending between 1976 and 1986 (a period in which we were not, incidentally, at war).

The program has promised, and historically delivered, a benefit that rises with wages in the economy. In order to maintain this commitment, we may have to increase the system's revenues at some point. Would this place an undue burden on the post-2034 labor force? Hardly. Even if we were to increase payroll taxes to cover the shortfall, the added cost would barely dent the average real wage in 2034, which will be over 30 percent higher than it is today. It takes a great deal of imagination to perceive this as some sort of highway robbery by tomorrow's senior citizens against the youth of today.

The simple truth is that our economy is generating more than enough income to provide a rising standard of living for future generations while meeting our commitments to Social Security. That's true even at the terribly slow rates of growth projected for the future.

The strength of the economy isn't perhaps as obvious as it should be, mainly because the majority of employees haven't been sharing in the gains from economic growth. For more than 20 years, most wage and salary earners have actually seen a real decline in their pay (Mishel, Bernstein, and Schmitt 1999). So when people hear that future generations will be able to meet Social Security's obligations out of a much higher income, they don't believe it.

To reclaim the majority's share of the economic pie is the real "challenge and opportunity of the twenty-first century," to paraphrase another of President Clinton's favorite lines. Yet the question of income distribution has been removed from the political agenda. Instead we are told that we can no longer afford our not-so-generous social safety net for the elderly. It is one of the greatest triumphs in the history of public relations to have transformed this prolonged episode of class warfare into an intergenerational conflict.

Mark Twain once said that a lie can get halfway around the world before the truth even gets its shoes on, and it's hard to find a more compelling example than the lie about Social Security's finances. Despite the fact that none of the numbers cited here are a matter of dispute, the public has been overwhelmingly convinced that Social Security is in deep trouble. According to a February 1998 poll by Peter Hart Research, 60 percent of nonretired Americans expect Social Security to pay much lower benefits or no benefits at all when they retire. The proportion is even higher, at 72 percent, for people aged 18–34.

Ironically, the only real threat to Social Security comes not from any fiscal or demographic constraints but from the political assaults on the program by would-be "reformers." If not for these attacks, the probability that Social Security "will not be there" when anyone who is alive today retires would be about the same as the odds that the U.S. government will not be there. The latter event is, of course, a possibility, but not enough of a likelihood that most people would plan their retirement around it.

Confusion over these issues is not confined to the general public: it has infiltrated the upper reaches of the economics profession as well. Lester Thurow is a former dean of MIT's Sloan School of Management, arguably one of the nation's best writers on economic topics. He is also to the left of most economists with regard to issues concerning the appropriate size and scope of government and its intervention in the economy. Yet in an essay in the *New York Times Magazine,* he argued that the nation's growing elderly population constituted "a new. . . revolutionary class, one that is bringing down the social welfare state, destroying government finances, altering the distribution of purchasing power and threatening the investments that all societies need to make to have a successful future" (Thurow 1996).[2]

Even Paul Krugman, one of the nation's foremost economists and winner of the John Bates Clark award (for the best economist under 40 years of age), fell victim to these popular notions of demographic determinism. In a favorable review of Peter G. Peterson's latest book, *Will America Grow Up Before It Grows Old?,* he endorsed the volume's thesis that major reform of the Social Security system was necessary to avoid an unresolvable budget

2. Among the misstatements that Thurow used to support his thesis was the assertion that "the current 15 percent Social Security tax rate would have to be boosted to 40 percent by 2029 to provide the benefits that have been promised." The current tax for Social Security (including Survivors and Disability Insurance) is 12.4 percent of payroll (6.2 percent for both employer and employee). According to the best projections of the Social Security trustees, this tax rate is sufficient to pay full benefits through 2034; these benefits could be maintained for the next 75 years (through 2074) with a 2.07 percent payroll tax increase—about 1 percent each for employer and employee.

crisis 20–30 years from now. "The budgetary effects of this demographic tidal wave are straightforward to compute, but so huge as to defy comprehension," he wrote (Krugman 1996a). Krugman later admitted, though, that he "went overboard in supporting Pete Peterson's position on entitlements and demographics. . . I broke my own rule that you should always check an argument both with a back-of-the-envelope calculation and by consulting with the real experts, no matter how plausible and reasonable its author sounds" (Krugman 1996b).

Both Krugman and Thurow fell for the "entitlements trick," a device deployed with great success by advocacy groups like Peterson's Concord Coalition. The idea is to lump Social Security and Medicare together as "entitlements for the elderly." On the basis of the last 30 years of health care inflation, it is easy to project explosive growth in future Medicare spending. The federal budget deficit therefore also explodes, and the whole economy goes down the tubes.

But Social Security and Medicare are separate programs, funded by separate taxes. There is a connection in that Medicare's Part A, which covers hospital insurance, was modeled after Social Security in the sense that it is a social insurance program for the elderly. Most people probably do not distinguish between the part of their payroll tax that goes to Social Security and the part that goes to Medicare. As a political matter, for example, a large increase in the payroll tax for one program would make people less willing to pay more for the other.

But the two programs are financed separately, and they face very different financial problems, with different causes. Although Social Security is not facing any serious financial difficulties, Medicare will run into serious trouble within the next decade if medical care inflation continues at its historic rates.

Because the fees paid by Medicare to health care providers are overwhelmingly determined in the private health care system, Medicare's financial problems have been driven by decades of double-digit inflation in the private sector. The program could be abolished entirely, but that would not avert the economic disaster 35 years from now that emerges from a simple projection of past increases in health care spending into the future. In short, past rates of increase in health care spending are economically unsustainable, regardless of what happens to Medicare (see chapter 3). These projections make a good argument for health care reform, but they say little about "entitlements for the elderly," and nothing at all about Social Security.

Introduction

The generational warriors have shunted aside these basic facts, preferring instead to view Medicare's real financing problems, like Social Security's imagined problems, through a fantastic prism of demographic determinism. Peter Peterson conjures up frightening dystopian visions of "a nation of Floridas" (Peterson 1996), with hordes of gray-haired baby boomers jetting around the country on senior citizen travel discounts, laying waste to the potential savings of Generations X, Y, and Z. The media have been influenced by these warnings, and we are regularly informed, as in the *New York Times*, that "Social Security faces a crisis early next century when the 76 million in the baby boom generation start retiring and putting a strain on the system" (Mitchell 1998).

But the baby boomers begin retiring in 2008, and at that time Social Security will still be running an annual surplus of about $150 billion (in constant 1999 dollars) per year. In fact the last of the baby boomers will already be retired by the time the system suffers its projected shortfall, even assuming the slow growth described above, at the end of 2034. It may come as a surprise to many readers that the main reason for this projected shortfall in the second half of the 75-year planning period is not the retirement of the baby boom generation. Actuarially, the main reason is that people are living longer.

Another example of how the truth of these matters can be so easily turned upside down is the belief of millions of people that Social Security has actually contributed to the federal budget deficits and the national debt. In fact the opposite is true: the Social Security trust fund loans its annual surplus, now running at over $124 billion, to the federal government. The surplus, which has been accumulating since 1983, when the payroll tax was increased, will help finance the baby boomers' retirement, which is why the program will not have any trouble meeting its obligations while the boomers are retiring.

So much for the "demographic time bomb" with which the system's "reformers" have been threatening us. With a few selected facts dressed up as surprises—such as a rising elderly population or a declining ratio of workers to retirees—and an oversized dose of verbal and accounting trickery, opponents of Social Security have been able to create the impression that the program is demographically unsustainable. This impression is false, as would be any economic projections that failed to take into account the other side of the equation, namely, the growth of the economy (see chapter 1).

Introduction

Even the financial problems of Medicare do not result, for the most part, from demographic changes. While it is true that older people, on average, require more health care than the young, overall health care spending, as a percentage of gross domestic product, does not necessarily have to increase with the average age of the population. In fact, among most developed countries there appears to be no correlation between health care spending and the percentage of the population that is over 65. As a percentage of our economy, we spend twice as much on health care as does Sweden, for example, yet 17.3 percent of Sweden's population is over 65, a proportion we will not reach for another 25 years (see chapter 3).

Rather, the financial threat to Medicare arises as this relatively more efficient system—its administrative costs are less than one-fourth those of the private system—is subjected to increasing "marketization." The number of senior citizens who get their Medicare coverage through health maintenance organizations (HMOs) more than tripled from 1992 to 1998 and has been growing at a rate of 25 percent per year. It doesn't take a financial genius at an HMO to figure out how to profit in this market. With about 90 percent of senior citizens costing Medicare an average of only $1,200 each, and with the government paying HMOs up to $6,000 per person, depending on the region, managed-care providers have been able to profit enormously by selecting, as much as possible, the healthiest senior citizens and leaving the rest (the least healthy 10 percent cost about $37,000 each) in the hands of Medicare. It all works out quite nicely for the HMOs, who can point to rising costs for Medicare relative to the more "efficient" private sector. Never mind that the HMOs' cost reductions are achieved not only through selection of healthier patients—wasting even more resources in the selection process—but also by cutting back on necessary medical procedures. The prejudice in favor of market-based solutions is so powerful that even the groundswell of consumer dissatisfaction has yet to force policymakers to reexamine it.

In the last few years, the spread of managed care has created the illusion of efficiency in the private sector by reducing private medical inflation to more manageable levels. It remains to be seen whether these lower levels of price increases can be sustained, particularly without further cuts in necessary medical services.[3] In the meantime, the call for real health care reform

3. Health insurance premiums are expected to increase by approximately 7 percent in 1999, as compared to overall inflation running at about 2.2 percent.

has been muted, and the country has been moving in the opposite direction from where it needs to go. While HMOs soak Medicare for its profitable patients and services, cuts are proposed to bring the program closer to fiscal balance. And recent legislation has opened the door to further fragmentation of the risk pool by allocating $2.2 billion to create "medical savings accounts." These would allow the healthiest among senior citizens to gamble that their health care expenses will be less than average and to keep some of the difference if they win.

Privatization fever has now spread to Social Security, fueled by the fastest run-up in stock prices in U.S. economic history.[4] Advocates have crafted their appeal to the growing segment of the public that has at least some money invested in stocks, mostly in 401(k) retirement plans. This is still a minority of the population—about 41 percent of households at latest count. And ownership is highly concentrated: the typical stock-owning household has only about $14,000, with millions holding only a very small proportion of their assets in stocks. At the other end of the distribution, about 5 percent of households hold the majority of stocks.

Nonetheless, there has been a rapid expansion in stock ownership, primarily through stock mutual funds, over the last decade. This growth has created a base of support for the idea that people could be better off if their Social Security payroll taxes were invested privately. According to various popular presentations of this idea, everyone could be a millionaire upon retirement.

And indeed they could, if stocks were to continue to double every three years. But there are limits to such speculative bubbles. The reality is that the very run-up in stock values that has placed privatization on the political agenda makes even the relatively modest returns of previous decades less likely in future years. Furthermore, due partly to a slowing of population growth and partly to a (largely unexplained) slowdown in the growth of productivity, the economy is not projected to grow as fast as it did previously. But neither the privatizers nor even the actuaries who made the projections for the recent Advisory Council on Social Security have taken these facts into account when projecting the rate of return for equities. This omission is strange, because it is only under the conditions of the very slow growth forecast that there is

---

4. Much more important than the bull market have been the longer-term political and ideological changes that have set the stage for the pro-privatization effort (see below).

even a small projected shortfall in Social Security's revenues. But if the economy is going to grow at less than half the rate of the past 75 years, as the Social Security trustees predict, then the return on equities cannot maintain its past performance.

Over the past 75 years, the stock market has averaged a real (after-inflation) annual return of 7 percent. This is a healthy rate, which would double an investor's money about every 10 years. Privatizers argue that the extra risks of the market smooth out over a long period of time, making the market the best place for retirement savings. And they complain that employees whose savings are primarily diverted to Social Security are unfairly prevented from cashing in on these higher returns. During the stock market's turbulence in 1997 and again in 1998, millions of small investors showed their faith in these arguments by buying during the dips and pushing the market back up. "I'm in it for the long haul" was a typical response by mutual fund owners to the market's wild ride.

But it is precisely the long haul that one can actually say something about. In the short run, all kinds of speculative bubbles are possible. Psychological factors—most obviously, the expectation of either higher earnings in the future or simply higher stock prices—can drive the stock market to seemingly unlimited heights. But over a long period of time—certainly well within the enormously long 75-year planning horizon for the Social Security system—the price of stocks is limited by the earnings of their underlying assets. That is, stocks are ultimately valuable because the companies they represent earn profits. These profits either are distributed to shareholders in the form of dividends or, if reinvested in the company, form the basis for shareholders' capital gains.

In the short run, there is no necessary relation between the price of stock shares and a company's profits: investors will continue buying so long as they think the price will be higher next year. And it will be higher as long as enough people believe that it will. But this process has an upper limit, as the Japanese learned all too well in 1990. At that time the Nikkei index of Japanese stocks had reached 38,712; it now stands below 14,000.

No one can safely predict when the stock market will reach its upper limit—anyone with such forecasting acumen could get rich overnight. But there are certain things we can pretty much rule out when we look at a long enough period of time. For example, the price-to-earnings ratios of stocks in the United States are now at near-record levels of 33 to 1. If prices continue to rise faster than profits, this ratio could go higher still. But would investors still hold stocks if it reached 234 to 1? It strains the imagination that they would, yet these are in fact the consequences of assuming that the market will continue to provide a 7 percent return. As noted above, returns on stocks depend on profits, and the growth of profits is proportional to the growth of the economy. If the economy grows at half its past rate, which is the assumption underlying the dire Social Security forecasts, then profits cannot grow as fast as they used to. And so, if we are to accept the projections of a 7 percent rate of return, we must also believe that the price of stocks will rise meteorically in relation to earnings. The arithmetic tells us that we would see a price-to-earnings ratio of 234 to 1 by 2055.

Undoubtedly the bubble would burst long before the price of stocks flew this far away from the earnings potential of the stocks' underlying assets. So we can safely conclude that the forecast of the privatizers (and of the Advisory Council on Social Security) of a 7 percent real rate of return on equities is, for all practical purposes, impossible. It turns out that the rate of return that is compatible with their projected economic growth is about 3.5 percent. Then there are the quite substantial costs of administration and brokerage fees that the current system avoids but that a private system couldn't. Adding these in knocks the return to privatized accounts down another percentage point, to 2.5 percent (see chapter 5).

And this is still a very charitable evaluation of privatization. Its advocates would like to maintain the mandatory character of Social Security while channeling this money into private accounts. They could hardly choose otherwise. Most households have not taken advantage of existing tax breaks for private savings. According to the most recent data available, of the 70.5 million workers with annual incomes under $30,000 in 1993, only 5.4 percent put money in an individual retirement account. Forcing people to save and invest their money in privatized accounts raises a host of interesting but not easily resolvable problems. The government will have to certify certain mutual funds for participation in this system. It will have to protect against fraud and other forms of abuse. There will be a lot of political pressure to bail out funds that go bankrupt. And will the government prevent people from borrowing against their forced savings? How will it enforce the conversion of these savings into a stream of retirement income?

Even if all these problems could be resolved at reasonable expense, and without creating an enormous, hateful bureaucracy, the big question remains:

what to do about all the people who have been promised Social Security payments over the next four decades? That's how long it will take for the first cohort of private Social Security investors to be able to retire on the returns from their individual accounts. In the meantime, while investors' money is going into these private accounts, the system cannot do much for the tens of millions of beneficiaries whose checks are due. That means a major tax increase, enough to guarantee a negative return for the first generations of privatized savers.

A number of other dubious arguments advanced in favor of privatization are addressed in chapter 5. These arguments have been put forward with increasing urgency as the privatizers struggle to achieve their goals before the public discovers that stock prices can go down as well as up.

Other "fixes" are on the table as well, all of which would cause enormous casualties among the elderly. For example, many people would like to raise the normal retirement age.[5] The idea might seem reasonable enough at first glance, since average life expectancy is increasing each decade. But consider what it means in light of the vast discrepancies in life expectancy among demographic groups. A typical black male worker who is 39 years old today can expect about 2.3 years of full retirement benefits, compared with 8.4 years for his white counterpart. Do we really want to drastically worsen that ratio by taking a year or more away from each?

Differences in life expectancy along class lines—income, occupation, and education—are about as big as the disparity by race. Raising the retirement age is therefore one of the most regressive ways to cut Social Security spending. It is analogous, in the realm of tax policy, to a per capita income tax increase. In other words, one could make the argument that since per capita income is growing every year, why not just increase everyone's tax bill by $1,000, regardless of his or her income or wealth? Such a proposal would never get serious consideration—it is much too regressive even for the advocates of a "flat tax" and similar schemes—yet this is essentially what we do through the Social Security system when we raise the retirement age among a population in which there is such a great disparity of retirement years.

---

5. The normal retirement age is the age at which people can retire with full benefits. It is currently 65 and will begin rising in the year 2000, reaching 67 for workers who retire in 2017. However, a majority of workers opt for early retirement, with a reduced benefit, at ages 62–64.

Other proposed fixes are similarly regressive, and unjustifiable on economic grounds, yet they seem to get serious attention. One of the more prominent of these (discussed in chapter 4) is the proposal to cut the Social Security cost-of-living adjustment (COLA), under the assumption that the consumer price index (CPI), on which COLAs are based, overstates the true rate of inflation (see Baker 1997). A panel of economists was appointed by the Senate in 1995 for the purpose of determining how much the CPI overstates inflation. The Boskin Commission, chaired by President Bush's former chief economist, Michael Boskin, decided that the CPI was off by 1.1 percentage points. This meant, or at least it was hoped, that Social Security's COLA could be cut by that amount. That may not sound like a lot, but if this conclusion had been adopted in 1998, the average beneficiary would have lost about $1,500 over the following five years.

Since America's poorest seniors rely the most heavily on Social Security, such changes would cause a significant increase in poverty among the elderly. If this change had been made 10 years ago, there would be at least 600,000 more senior citizens in poverty now than there are currently (Weisbrot 1997, 20–21).

Supporters would like to dress these measures up in a white coat of "technical expertise," but that coat looks rather shabby on closer inspection. The most serious problem is that adopting the Boskin Commission's estimate of inflation would require us to radically change our view of the economy. For example, if we have been overstating inflation by as much as the commission claims, then real income has been growing a lot faster than we thought—so fast, in fact, that most Americans must have been living near or below the poverty level in 1960 (a year in which 57 percent of households owned their own homes and 76 percent had cars). Furthermore, the whole history of declining real wages for the majority of workers over the last two decades will also need to be rewritten—conveniently for some—as an illusion.

Looking toward the future, we get even more interesting results if we accept the commission's estimate. It means not only that we have underestimated real wage growth in the past but that we are similarly off the mark in forecasting the future. The Boskin future is so bright that the typical wage earner will be hauling in more than $50,000 a year in real (inflation-adjusted) income by 2030, or about twice the typical wage in 1995. The irony of this effort to redo the CPI is that, if its proponents are correct, their rationale for cutting Social Security benefits disappears. We would be cutting benefits for those who spent most of their lives in poverty in order to maintain lower taxes on generations who will have, by even today's standards, quite healthy incomes. Even the most shameless granny-bashers should have a hard time justifying this kind of redistribution.

Other numbers in the Boskin report don't make much sense either. To take just one example: the commission argues that the CPI doesn't adequately take into account quality improvements, such as better gas mileage or the installation of air bags in cars. But the Bureau of Labor Statistics (BLS) makes extensive adjustments for quality. In 1995, the CPI rose 1.8 percent; without the quality adjustments made by the BLS, it would have risen 4.0 percent. This is a large adjustment, but the Boskin Commission, without conducting any original research on the subject, asserts that this is not enough. Their arguments are not convincing. In the case of cars, the BLS asks auto companies how much of their price increases are due to quality improvements. It is hard to imagine that these companies would respond with severe understatements.

The Boskin Commission was stacked with five economists who had previously proclaimed their belief that the CPI seriously overstates inflation. They looked for everything that might support this conclusion while overlooking evidence and arguments that pointed in the opposite direction. The scenario is a sad illustration of what happens when those pursuing a political agenda— in this case the Senate Finance Committee—attempt to corrupt the process of estimating fundamental economic statistics.

Congress has thus far failed to incorporate the Boskin changes, but the issue is far from settled. Indeed, one of the more prominent Social Security "reform" proposals on the table right now, put forth by Senator Daniel Patrick Moynihan, contains a COLA cut.

Social Security and Social Insurance

Social Security is our largest and most successful antipoverty program, keeping about half of the nation's senior citizens from falling below the official poverty line (SSA 1998b). In 1959, the poverty rate among the elderly was more than 35 percent; by 1970, it was twice the rate of that for the general population. Largely as a result of the Social Security program, it has since fallen to 10.8 percent, or slightly less than that for the general population (SSA 1997). For two-thirds of the elderly, Social Security makes up the majority of their income; for the poorest 16 percent, it is their only source of income (SSA 1998b).

Introduction

Social Security provides about $12 trillion worth of life insurance, more than that provided by the entire private life insurance industry (Ball et al. 1997, 32). The program's 44 million beneficiaries today include 7 million survivors of deceased workers, about 1.4 million of whom are children (SSA 1998a, 1). Some 5.5 million people receive disability benefits, including not only disabled workers but also their dependents. For a typical employee, the value of the insurance provided by the program would be more than $200,000 for disability and about $300,000 for survivors insurance (Ball et al. 1997, 32).

The coverage of the program is nearly universal—about 95 percent of senior citizens either are receiving benefits or will be eligible to receive them upon retirement (Advisory Council 1997, 88). For a society that wants to ensure some minimum standard of living for its elderly, this is an important achievement in itself. But it also allows for other accomplishments that would be difficult or impossible to replicate in the private sector. For example, Social Security provides an inflation-proof, guaranteed annuity from the time of retirement for the rest of the beneficiary's life. The cost of retirement, survivors, and disability insurance does not depend on the individual's health or other risk factors. And the benefits are portable from job to job, unlike many employer-sponsored pension plans.

The success of Social Security also owes much to the superior economic efficiency of social insurance as a means of providing core retirement income. The program's administrative costs are a small fraction of the private alternatives: they amount to less than 1 percent of payout (SSA 1996a), as opposed to 12–14 percent for the private life insurance industry.[6] On these strictly economic grounds alone, the case for Social Security is strong.

But social insurance also embodies a different ethic and a different conception of the relation between the individual and society. The ethic is a solidaristic one, which is different from either self-interest or altruism. It transcends this dichotomy in favor of a collective self-interest that promotes the advancement of everyone.

Most of us will grow old and will, either before or during that time, experience health problems or reduced capacity for work. The ethic of social insurance says that "we are all in this together" and that it is in our collective and individual interest to pitch in and provide for these eventualities and risks. We can contribute when we are relatively young, healthy, and working,

6. Based on data from the American Council of Life Insurance.

and draw benefits when we are not. Some will draw a luckier number in the genetic lottery or inherit wealth or even be more successful or healthy or live longer by virtue of their own efforts or wisdom; but this is no reason to deny the necessities of life to anyone else, any more than we would want our local fire department to ignore calls from the poor, or even from those whose fires were caused by their own carelessness.

The case for social insurance is also grounded in a view of society that differs considerably from the agglomeration of atomized individuals, each maximizing his or her own utility, that forms the foundation of contemporary neoclassical microeconomics. In this broader context, the national product is seen more as a social product, which requires the efforts and cooperation of all who work. Market outcomes are not necessarily fair or just, nor should they determine one's fate, especially in times of hardship.

Despite the political resurgence of a market-driven ethic in the last two decades, the majority sentiment is probably still closer to the solidaristic ethic embodied in the principles of social insurance. At the very least, this is true for the areas that social insurance has typically covered: protection against the reduced earnings potential and hardships of old age, sickness, disability, and unemployment.

Social insurance has also succeeded in avoiding the stigma and political weaknesses from which means-tested welfare programs have suffered. These weaknesses have been increasingly exploited by politicians since the 1980s, culminating in the elimination of Aid to Families With Dependent Children (AFDC) in 1996. Programs like Social Security and Medicare have been protected from these types of divisive attacks, largely due to their universal coverage and work-based entitlement.

Social Security has also become increasingly important in light of what has happened to the other two major sources of retirement income: private savings and employer-sponsored pension plans. The regressive changes in income distribution that have taken place over the last two decades have made it increasingly difficult for most people to save for their own retirement. The median wage actually fell 6.8 percent from 1973 to 1997, and declines have been much worse for those with less education. This is a drastic change from the previous era, from 1947 to 1973, when the typical wage earner saw real gains on the order of 79 percent (Mishel, Bernstein, and Schmitt 1997, 140–43; 1999, 131).

At the same time, private pensions have shifted from defined-benefit plans to defined-contribution plans. In a defined-benefit plan, the employer assumes the risk associated with the return on accumulated pension funds by guaranteeing a specified benefit upon retirement. In defined-contribution plans, such as 401(k) plans, which allow employees to defer compensation tax-free into retirement accounts, the employee assumes the risk. In the past, defined-benefit plans were the norm: 94 percent of those receiving private pension benefits today receive them through defined-benefit plans. But today more employees participate in defined-contribution plans than in defined-benefit plans. Together with the difficulty of saving for retirement out of declining real wages, these trends have made Social Security the one part of retirement income that the majority of Americans can really count on.

All of this makes a strong case for expanding, rather than shrinking, social insurance, especially if we want to counter the now decades-old trends toward increasing inequality and poverty in the United States. As noted in chapter 3, the health care system would be a logical next step in such an expansion. Medicare was an attempt to extend the principles of social insurance to health care, but only partially, since the elderly are still segmented from the rest of the population. Insurance involves the pooling of risk, and from an economic standpoint the most efficient way to do this is to put everyone in one large risk pool. Together with the enormous economies of scale in administration, this is the basis for the superior efficiency of social insurance.

Although Medicare has succeeded in providing access to health care for millions of older Americans and in reducing administrative costs relative to private insurance, it has not been able to contain the explosive medical price pressures that have been generated by the private sector. The rational solution would seem to be to extend social insurance for health care to the rest of the population, thereby eliminating enormous amounts of waste and placing global controls on overall spending. The administrative savings alone, according to some estimates, would be enough to provide health care coverage to the 43 million Americans who are currently uninsured. But it will be difficult to have an informed public debate about the expansion of social insurance as long as widespread misconceptions prevail about our existing programs of Social Security and Medicare.

The Politics of Non-issues

As will be seen throughout this book, the numerous cuts proposed to "fix" Social Security are neither just nor justifiable, nor are they necessary. The system's financing problems are still very much in the distant future. Should they materialize, they would be quite small relative to the nation's future income.

How is it that a sense of urgency has been created around such a small, far-off, nonproblem? Multiple causes have led to this strange result, ranging from the crass commercial interests of Wall Street, to more general political trends, to recent changes in the esoteric world of economic theory.

There is no doubt that Wall Street has an enormous direct stake in any kind of privatization of Social Security, and it has been investing in the production of ideas necessary to bring this transition about. "You could be staring at 130 million new accounts," said William Shipman of State Street Global Advisors, a division of State Street Bank, which has contributed tens of thousands of dollars to various research institutes to study privatization. One-quarter of the Cato Institute's $2 million Project on Social Security Privatization has come from Wall Street firms (Lieberman 1997).

But the potential windfall of a privatized system is only part of the financiers' interest in the reform of Social Security. The big bondholders have a financial stake in anything that reduces federal spending or, for that matter, growth and employment generally. They have only one enemy: inflation. And like those who suffer from obsessive-compulsive disorder, they see pitfalls and dangers where others see only the normal vicissitudes of everyday life, or even progress: in lower unemployment rates, rising wages, and, for the longer term, a rising share of national income devoted to federal entitlements.

The bondholders' perspective has been so thoroughly assimilated that much of current policy discussion implicitly assumes that what's good for the bond market is good for the economy, even when that means higher unemployment and slower growth. Thus we are regularly informed in the business press that the Federal Reserve Board "will have to raise interest rates" if wages continue rising (Stevenson 1998c), even at the rate of productivity growth, as if there were no choices that would allow the majority of wage earners to get a proportionate share of the gains from an expanding economy.

The attention that has been devoted in recent years to the problem of balancing the federal budget provides another example of the triumph of ideology over economic reasoning. It is also a good illustration of how the politics of non-issues has come to dominate civil society in the United States. Here is an economic policy that, even if we grant all the dubious assumptions of its proponents (for example, that the economy normally runs at full employment) can only be regarded as trivial in its effects. Just look at the difference between running a budget deficit of 2.5 percent of gross domestic product (GDP)—more than $200 billion in today's economy—versus balancing the budget every year from 1996 until 2030. According to the Congressional Budget Office, the best that balancing the budget could do for us would be to give us the output of goods and services in 2030 that we would not otherwise have until 2031. As a best-case scenario, it's not much to write home about.

To illustrate the relative insignificance of the economic impact of balancing the budget, consider the impact of past and current trends toward increasing inequality in the distribution of income. If these trends continue to 2030, they will cost the typical family about 25 percent of its income. Yet no legislative agenda, constitutional amendment, or campaign for high office has been centered on this very real and continuing threat to the well-being of future generations. Instead we have been treated to the dire premonitions of the generational warriors, who fortunately remain, at this writing, generals without an army. Nonetheless, they have managed to exert more influence than those who are concerned about more contemporary issues such as poverty and inequality. Their vehicles have included the academic writings of respected economists (see chapter 2), as well as popular writings and organizations such as Economic Security 2000, the Concord Coalition, and the Third Millennium. Through these efforts they have added their own special contribution to the litany of demographic determinism that has muddled the debate over entitlements for the elderly. That contribution has been to characterize the national debt as an unjust burden passed on to future generations, who will have to pay for our high living with a lifetime tax burden that will devour most of their hard-earned income.

The first part of the argument is based on a logical error: it is impossible for the present generation to "burden" future generations with a national debt.[7] Any debt owed *by* future generations will also be owed *to* future generations, because each generation that pays interest on the national debt pays

---

7. The exception to this generalization would be if current borrowing drove up interest rates enough to "crowd out" a large amount of private investment, thus leaving future

that money to members of the same generation who own the Treasury bonds. So the national debt, however much one may dislike it for aesthetic or other reasons, cannot be used as an instrument to redistribute income between generations.

The economists among the generational warriors will admit this if pressed (they do, after all, teach introductory economics courses) and retreat to other arguments. These arguments have been refined into a system of "generational accounting" that purports to show lifetime net tax rates averaging more than 80 percent for all future generations. However, as shown in chapter 2, some very special assumptions are required in order to reach this terrifying conclusion. One of those we have already seen: that public sector health care costs continue to rise without containment, based on past rates of increase. As noted above, such explosive rates of increase would wreak havoc by the middle of the next century, regardless of whether the government attempts to maintain its Medicare and Medicaid programs for the elderly and the poor. Such projections tell us less about questions of intergenerational equity than they do about the value of making projections based on unsustainable trends. If this is what we want to do for entertainment, we could forecast that more than a quarter of all American adults will be incarcerated, on parole, or on probation by 2045, based on past rates of increase in the number of people convicted of crimes.

It may seem strange that anyone would project such explosive health care costs into the indefinite future and focus only on the implications for people's tax burdens, but some of the other assumptions of generational accounting— such as unusually large discounting of future income, and treating education as a cost with no benefits—make even less economic or logical sense. When all of these assumptions are restored to normalcy, the whole nightmarish tax burden dreamed up by the generational accountants disappears (see chapter 2).

How can we explain the predominance of non-issues like the national debt, the federal budget deficit, generational accounting, and the Social Security "crisis," which cannot withstand the most minimal scrutiny through the lens of logic or empirical evidence? Part of the problem lies deep within our political system, and especially its corruption in the financing of election

---

generations with a much reduced capital stock. However, as noted above, the potential "crowding-out" effects of government borrowing turn out to be very small.

campaigns. In such a system it becomes nearly impossible for politicians to attack more real and urgent problems such as poverty and inequality. Those who attempt to do so soon discover that they cannot raise the ever-increasing amounts of money needed to make a serious bid for political office. At the same time we have experienced a major shift in the parameters of policy analysis, fallout from the years of antigovernment rhetoric and ideology of the Reagan era. Many of the core elements of this shift have been accepted by liberals and conservatives alike. The idea that the government cannot do anything right, or at least not as efficiently as the private sector, has become a truism.

All of these developments have thrust this particular set of non-issues into a prominent place in American politics. They have also found a more hospitable environment than they would have encountered 25 years ago, thanks to certain changes in the mainstream of economic theory. Central to the current debate is the idea that Americans are not saving enough and that this is a major cause of our economic problems. For example, the steep decline in the rate of growth of productivity—and hence in the growth of our economy and wages—is often attributed to a shortage of savings. This leads, according to the now conventional wisdom, to a lower rate of investment and therefore growth.

But this chain of causality running from savings behavior to investment to growth, which dominated economic theory prior to John Maynard Keynes and the Great Depression, has been rehabilitated only relatively recently. As explained in chapter 7, it is also possible to view the causality in the opposite direction: lower levels of investment result in lower productivity growth, which reduces the rate of growth of income. Savings rates then fall as a consequence, rather than a cause, of slower income growth. This view, which also relies on the more plausible assumption that our economy is not generally at full employment, was the predominant view among economists until about 25 years ago. The reincarnation of nineteenth-century macroeconomics in academia over the last couple of decades has done much to give these "shortage of savings" arguments a new lease on life. However, as noted above, even within the framework of such theories, increasing the savings rate by any amount that is within the realm of possibility would have almost no noticeable effect on growth. But that has not stopped the popularizers of Social Security and budget "reform" from drawing momentous conclusions. "To avoid steep economic decline," warns the Concord Coalition's Peter Peterson, "we must forsake our consumption and deficit habits and once again reshape ourselves as a savings-and-investment society" (Peterson 1996, 17).

This is a simple and attractive explanation for declining living standards. It appeals to traditional values of hard work, self-sacrifice, and thrift. Peterson likes to talk about his Greek immigrant parents, who arrived here penniless, operated a small restaurant that was open 24 hours a day, 365 days a year, and saved every nickel they could. There is also a significant and growing sector of the population that believes that Americans consume too much.[8] The reasons range from considerations of environmental sustainability to the sense that spending habits are forcing people to work many more hours than is necessary or desirable. Although these concerns do not necessarily overlap with the question of savings (we could, for example, reduce the workweek or the environmental "throughput" involved in consumption), they have made it easier to sell people on the idea that Americans should save more. Privatizers have added yet another layer of confusion by pretending that a system of personal retirement accounts would somehow increase the national savings rate. To the extent that taxes would have to be increased to pay for the transition, this would be true by definition. But that is not what they are saying, since they are not openly advocating increasing national savings by increasing taxes.

The current preoccupation with these non-issues is a transitory phenomenon. Like other intellectual fads it will spend its hour on the stage and then fade, freeing policymakers, politicians, think tanks, and journalists to turn their attention to more important concerns. In 1960 the poverty rate for American children was 27 percent. It fell to 14 percent in 1973, but by 1993 it was back up to 23 percent, eliminating most of the gains of the War on Poverty. Forty-three million people are without health insurance, and the numbers are still growing. Our educational system is failing to provide millions of children with even basic reading skills. And even middle-class families are struggling to put their children through college.

It is well within our means to solve these problems. In fact, most of them do not exist at anywhere near the same level in other industrialized countries of comparable income. Perhaps we should put these more pressing problems first on the agenda, and leave the phony crises for later.

---

8. In a 1995 poll by the Merck Family Fund, 82 percent of respondents acknowledged that "most of us buy and consume far more than we need" (Merck Family Fund 1995).

1 Social Security and Its Critics

THERE IS AN OLD RIDDLE that illustrates the kind of verbal and accounting trickery that has been used to create the illusion of a Social Security crisis. It goes like this: A man walks into a hotel and gives the clerk $30 for a room. The room costs $25, but the man takes off to his room without the change. The clerk summons an employee, gives him $5, and tells him to take it up to the guy's room. On the way up in the elevator, the employee decides to take $2, figuring he can tell the customer that the room costs $27. He gives the customer $3 and heads off to buy a drink.

Here's the punch line that has confused (at least temporarily) generations of listeners: the customer paid $27, the employee took $2—that adds up to $29. What happened to the last dollar?

Of course there is no missing dollar. The riddle is designed to make the listener think that there is a dollar missing by posing a question that at first glance appears to be part of a logical accounting framework. But in fact it is not.

It may seem incredible that the widespread belief in Social Security's "looming insolvency" has been generated by this kind of sleight of hand, but that is more or less the case. With enough money and power behind them, all sorts of ideas can find themselves promoted to the status of conventional wisdom—we should be thankful that no moneyed interests have yet thrown their weight into the search for the missing dollar. As for Social Security, the best way to sort out the truth of the matter is to look at the actual state of the system's finances, including projections into the future, and then see how the system's opponents (and "reformers") have misrepresented this picture.

Social Security's Finances

It is important to understand that the debate over the state of Social Security's finances is not an argument about what kind of economic assumptions to make about the future. That is, the most prominent voices on all sides of the issue—even those arguing for severe benefit cuts or privatization—are operating from the same set of economic and demographic assumptions about what will happen over the next 75 years. This may seem strange, because even relatively small changes in such variables as productivity or population growth, wage growth, and others can have a large effect on the projected balance sheet a few decades from now. But Social Security's critics have not seen fit to challenge the projections that are put together by the actuaries at the Social Security Administration. (These are updated and published each year in the annual report of the Board of Trustees of the Social Security trust fund.)

The trustees' report contains three sets of projections: a high-cost, intermediate-cost, and low-cost scenario. The intermediate projections—considered by the trustees to be their best estimates—are generally accepted as common ground in policy circles. When one looks at the assumptions, it is easy to see why even Social Security's most fervent opponents rarely try to make the case for anything worse.

The trustees' intermediate projections are based on a slow-growing economy, in fact worse than any previous period in American economic history. The economy is projected to grow at just under 1.5% per year over the 75-year planning horizon, far below the 3.0% growth rate of the last 75 years.

Even under these pessimistic assumptions, the Social Security system, without changing anything in the tax or benefit payout structure, will meet its obligations for the next 35 years. During this time the entire baby boom generation will retire, beginning with early retirees (at age 62) in the year 2008. Table 1-1 shows the projected number of beneficiaries over the trustees' planning period. The retirement of the baby boom generation can be seen in the sharp increase between 2010 and 2030, from 44.3 million to 70 million, or 58%. The two decades after that, by comparison, show only an 8.5% increase. But the retirement of the baby boomers has already been taken into account, and so the program will not have any trouble accommodating the flood of retirees during the 2010–30 period (as discussed below). This is in sharp contrast to widely held beliefs that the retirement of the baby boom generation will bankrupt Social Security.

Social Security and Its Critics

Table 1-1. Projected Social Security Beneficiaries, 1998–2075

Calendar year	Beneficiaries (thousands)
1999	38,139
2000	38,421
2005	40,485
2008	42,338
2010	44,332
2015	50,495
2020	57,905
2025	64,696
2030	69,960
2035	73,073
2040	74,073
2045	74,698
2050	75,913
2055	78,063
2060	80,521
2065	82,531
2070	84,198
2075	85,782

Source: Office of the Chief Actuary, Social Security Administration (April 9, 1999).
Note: Monthly benefits in current-payment status as of December 31. Based on intermediate-cost assumptions of Social Security trustees (SSA 1999).

The high level of financial security that the system now enjoys is not well appreciated. In 1983, the Social Security trust fund was within a few months of falling short on its obligations to beneficiaries. Of course no one came close to missing a check, and it is doubtful that the federal government would ever default on its obligations to beneficiaries simply because of a shortfall in the program's revenues. But in any case we are at least 35 years away from reaching the situation that we faced in 1983.

Few programs even a fraction of this size, public or private, can claim to be fully funded for more than the next three decades. That ought to be the end of the story—we have plenty of time to "fix" Social Security if it looks like it will run into trouble further up the road. But there are two main reasons why the story does not end here. The first is legal and technical: the trustees are required to show that the system is "in actuarial balance" for the next 75 years. As a practical matter, projections that far into the future are little more than fortune-telling. Think of the world in 1924—what possible conception of today's economy would anyone have had back then? Computers, air travel, mass electronic media, and popular ownership of cars had yet to enter the equation, not to mention the Great Depression and another world war. It strains credibility to imagine that we have any better idea what the world is going to look like 75 years from today. Nonetheless, that is the current law, and so the debate over Social Security is embedded in a 75-year planning period.

The second reason that three decades of solvency are not treated as well as they should be is political. In a climate of suspicion toward government programs in general, and with all the hype about entitlements, it is easy to find a credulous audience that will take 75-year projections seriously, especially if the projections show a shortfall, as they do, between year 35 and year 75. Yet even that shortfall, which may never materialize, is hardly anything to worry about. If we were to ignore the problem completely for the next 13 years and then fix it by the most politically drastic means—raising the payroll tax—future generations would not be greatly burdened. For example, an increase in the payroll tax of one-tenth of 1 percent each year (split between employer and employee), beginning in 2011 and continuing until 2046, would close the gap. This would still leave future generations with an after-tax wage far higher than that of today's employees. For example, the average employee in 2030 would have an after-tax wage that is 28.7 percent higher than today, in real (inflation-adjusted) terms. Without these payroll tax increases, that employee would have an average wage 30.7 percent higher than his or her counterpart of today. This is *real*, after-tax income, and it will be earned after the entire baby boom generation retires, with no cuts in benefits. This is hardly the stuff with which to send an army of generational warriors into the battlefield.

Moreover, changes recently made by the Bureau of Labor Statistics in the way it calculates the consumer price index (CPI) will extend Social Security's solvency further into the future. Some of these changes were recently incorporated into the trustees' projections, which helped push the date of depletion of the trust fund two years further out, to 2034. There are other changes in the CPI that have been made over the last three years that have not been fully incorporated into the trustees' projections. According to the Council of Economic Advisors, these changes would lower the measured rate of inflation by another 0.29 percentage points; the Congressional Budget Office has made similar estimates. If these changes were fully incorporated, the trust fund would remain solvent beyond 2043. (A lower inflation measurement boosts the trust fund because it means that both real wages—and thus the payroll taxes collected on them—and the real interest earned on the trust fund balance will be higher than expected.)

There are other, nontechnical reasons to challenge the *policies* on which the trustees' projections are based. That is, their projections (aside from the preceding technical issues) may well be the best available forecast of the future economic conditions that will determine the revenue and payouts of the Social Security system, based on past and current trends, but the trends themselves may be challenged on political-economic grounds. For example, the trustees' intermediate projections assume an unemployment rate of 6 percent persisting throughout the period. Until four years ago, most economists considered the "non-accelerating-inflation rate of unemployment" (NAIRU), sometimes referred to as the natural rate of unemployment, to be 6 percent, meaning that, if unemployment were to drop below 6 percent, inflation would accelerate. The Federal Reserve Board was guided by this view in conducting monetary policy. But unemployment has been below 6 percent for several years in the late 1990s—often below 5 percent—while at the same time inflation has actually fallen.

There is now a strong case for abandoning the concept of NAIRU altogether, and indeed if we look at it historically, economists' definition of the natural rate of unemployment has tended to follow the actual rate. In any case, it is clear that a considerably lower rate of unemployment than previously thought possible without accelerating inflation is indeed feasible, and it is within the power of the Federal Reserve Board to make it a reality.

Similarly, we might question whether the 1.3 percent productivity growth projected by the trustees is unalterable. Again, the problem is not in the trustees' projections but in the notion that the underlying trend should be accepted. From 1948 to 1973, productivity grew at an annual rate of 2.5 percent. The sharp drop since then (to 1.2 percent) has drastically narrowed the economic possibilities for all affected generations. After all, it is rising productivity—output per unit of labor—that is the source of rising living standards. Economists do not agree on an explanation for the slowdown, but clearly there are policy changes that might affect the rate of productivity growth. One is the rate of growth of wages. Although rising productivity is a source of wage increases, the causality also runs in the opposite direction. Throughout much of its economic history, the United States had higher wages than Europe, and this gave employers an incentive to substitute capital for labor, which increases the productivity of labor. This increasing substitution of capital for labor is associated with more rapid technological change generally, since the new machinery almost always embodies more advanced technology than the old.

One problem we have in the present period is that the availability of labor at low and stagnating wages discourages this productivity-enhancing investment. It allows employers to create new jobs that have low levels of productivity, because they can pay low wages. The creation of these low-productivity, low-wage jobs slows the overall rate of growth of productivity in the economy.

It is commonly believed, especially in the popular literature, that rapid technological change leads to higher unemployment. But this is not true, either logically or historically. So long as macroeconomic policy is oriented toward full employment, technological change and its accompanying increases in productivity need not increase unemployment at the level of the whole economy. During the late 1960s, for example, when productivity was growing more than twice as fast as it is today, unemployment dropped to 3.5–3.8 percent (*ERP* 1998, table B-42). And the whole Bretton Woods era (1946–73) had considerably lower unemployment than the years since (4.7 percent vs. 6.8 percent), with vastly higher productivity growth (Mishel, Bernstein, and Schmitt 1999, 221).

It is therefore possible to have higher wage growth, faster productivity growth, and lower unemployment than we enjoy currently or assume in our economic projections. Such changes could not only balance Social Security's finances but also allow us to address some of the nation's more real economic problems. Moreover, all this is aside from the more pressing issues of the increase in wage inequality and the shift in income distribution from wages to profits, which are at least as vital to the debate.

It is a sad testimony to the intellectual emptiness of contemporary debates over economic issues that policies that have stunted our growth and continue to limit our possibilities for the future are taken—mostly unconsciously—as fixed. The source of our economic problems is then located in unalterable exogenous factors like demography or factors that are probably better understood as "dependent variables," such as the savings behavior of individuals. It would seem to make more sense to push for policies that would result in higher wage and productivity growth and lower unemployment than to take the performance of the last two decades as our inevitable fate for the first three-quarters of the twenty-first century—and then obsess about the small possible gap in Social Security financing that might result. But myths can have a power that is greater than reality, and the myth of demography as destiny, in conjunction with others, has put the entitlement cutters in the driver's seat.

Social Security and Its Critics

It must be emphasized that, however sensible and beneficial it would be to change the underlying growth trends in productivity, employment, and wages, the soundness of Social Security's financing does not depend on any such improvements in the overall economy. Throughout this book we accept, for the sake of argument, the trustees' intermediate cost projections and their underlying (rather pessimistic) assumptions. Should the predicted financing gap actually materialize, it would not necessarily have to be closed by a flat payroll tax increase. But in any case it is nothing to worry about. To understand the current debate it is necessary to examine, in some detail, the devices by which this potential molehill up the road has been transformed into a mountain in the middle of our backyard—indeed, if one is to believe the critics, a volcano that is about to erupt and bury our children and grandchildren under a suffocating burden of intergenerational income transfers.

The Disappearing Trust Fund

One of the most important efforts of Social Security's critics has been to undermine public confidence in the program's solvency. This brings them halfway to their goal, since people are less likely to defend the program from privatization or other changes if they don't think they have much of a stake in it. The critics' success can be measured by the number of times the words "looming insolvency" are used to describe the system's finances (see, e.g., Stevenson 1998b). "Looming" is a strong adjective to use for an event that won't occur until 2014, when benefits paid out are projected to exceed taxes received, but 2014 is a lot closer than 2034, which is how long it takes for the trustees' projections to show a shortfall. These guideposts have contributed to the widespread belief that the Social Security system will go broke when the baby boomers begin to retire, and so a closer look at this problem is important, and will provide a convenient way to illustrate some of the basics of the system.

Social Security is a pay-as-you-go system in that money taken from people's paychecks, as well as employers' contributions, goes to pay current retirees. This arrangement causes no small amount of indigestion among the system's conservative opponents, who would prefer a "fully funded" system that, much like a pension plan, would rely on an established pool of funds invested in financial assets. Benefits to retirees would be paid out of the returns generated by the fund's assets.

Primarily to prepare for the retirement of the baby boom generation, the Social Security trust fund has been building up a surplus since 1984. It currently stands at more than $800 billion and is now growing by about $100 billion a year. In order to get a return on this money, the trustees buy U.S. government bonds earning about 6.4 percent a year. These are perhaps the safest investment available in the world today.

The first baby boomers will begin to retire about 2008. As can be seen in table 1-2, by 2014 the benefits paid by the system will be slightly greater than the money coming in from payroll taxes. The "reformers" argue on this basis that Social Security will be in trouble in 2014 (see, e.g., Urban Institute 1998, fig. 7). But this is like saying that Bill Gates would have trouble paying his mortgage if he left his job at Microsoft. At the end of 2014, the fund will have nearly $2.3 trillion in assets (in today's dollars), and it will be receiving $138 billion in interest payments on top of its income from payroll taxes. In fact, the combined interest income and payroll taxes ($723 billion) will exceed benefit payments by $130 billion. With this contribution from interest payments, the fund will be able to pay all benefits out of its income until 2022. From that point until 2034, it will be able to maintain full benefit payments by drawing on the principal in the trust fund.

The alarmists are not so easily turned back. "But," they object, "when the trust fund cashes in its bonds, the government will have to find money somewhere. So Social Security—or some other spending—will have to be cut." On this basis they dismiss the trust fund's assets as "mere pieces of paper" or "the government owing money to itself." Dubbed merely an accounting fiction, the trust fund vanishes. And so does the distinction between Social Security payroll taxes and the rest of government revenue. It's all just one big pot of money coming in, and one pot of money pouring out.

While it is indeed true that the government will have to borrow from other sources as the Social Security surplus shrinks, its need to borrow has nothing to do with the solvency of the Social Security system. One way to see this is to imagine that the Social Security trust fund were invested in private stocks and bonds rather than government bonds. When the system's payouts begin to exceed its income, the fund would begin cashing in its portfolio, and the proceeds would be used to help pay benefits, right up to 2034. Since this money would come from the private sector, no one could claim that the federal budget was being strained by Social Security spending.[1] It is difficult to

---

1. It is worth noting that the difference between the income of the trust fund and its obligations in 2022 amounts to 1.0 percent of gross domestic product (GDP), increasing to

Social Security and Its Critics

Table 1-2. Estimated Operations of the Combined Old-Age and Survivors Insurance and Disability Insurance Trust Funds in Constant 1999 Dollars, 1999–2033 (in billions)

Calendar year	Income excluding interest	Interest income	Total income	Outgo	Assets at end of year
1999	464.3	54.1	518.3	394.0	886.8
2000	469.4	57.7	527.1	400.7	995.1
2001	477.7	62.0	539.7	408.3	1,102.5
2002	484.7	66.8	551.4	417.6	1,208.5
2003	492.0	71.8	563.8	426.9	1,313.1
2004	499.0	77.0	576.0	436.7	1,414.0
2005	507.8	82.7	590.5	447.4	1,514.0
2006	515.7	88.6	604.2	459.1	1,612.1
2007	525.0	94.7	619.7	471.4	1,709.7
2008	533.0	101.0	634.0	484.4	1,804.8
2009	542.1	107.9	649.9	499.8	1,897.3
2010	551.3	114.6	665.9	516.0	1,986.6
2011	560.0	121.3	681.3	533.0	2,071.3
2012	568.3	127.8	696.1	551.6	2,149.6
2013	576.7	133.9	710.7	571.7	2,220.0
2014	585.0	137.9	722.9	592.7	2,279.3
2015	593.2	141.2	734.4	614.8	2,326.1
2016	601.2	143.6	744.8	638.0	2,358.6
2017	609.2	145.2	754.4	662.0	2,375.6
2018	617.2	145.7	762.9	686.7	2,376.0
2019	625.2	145.2	770.4	712.3	2,358.2
2020	633.1	143.6	776.7	738.0	2,321.6
2021	640.7	140.8	781.5	763.1	2,265.8
2022	648.7	136.8	785.5	787.7	2,191.3
2023	656.3	131.7	788.0	812.0	2,097.3
2024	663.9	125.4	789.3	836.0	1,983.6
2025	671.7	117.8	789.5	859.4	1,850.4
2026	679.5	109.2	788.6	882.3	1,697.6
2027	687.3	99.2	786.5	904.6	1,525.3
2028	695.3	88.2	783.5	925.7	1,334.3
2029	703.7	76.0	779.7	946.0	1,125.4
2030	712.2	62.7	774.9	965.2	899.2
2031	720.8	48.4	769.2	983.8	655.9
2032	729.5	33.0	762.5	1,001.8	395.6
2033	738.2	16.6	754.9	1,018.7	119.1

Source: Office of the Chief Actuary, Social Security Administration (April 9, 1999).
Note: Based on intermediate-cost assumptions of Social Security trustees (SSA 1999).

1.6 percent of GDP in 2027 (it is likely that revenues would be increased by then) and 1.9 percent in 2033. These would represent significant but not extremely high levels of borrowing; the federal budget deficit in 1983, for example, was 6.1 percent of GDP. But for those who consider this to be a serious problem, it is important to clarify that the source of the problem lies outside Social Security, and that the fact that the Social Security system has loaned its

see why the composition of the trust fund's portfolio should make any difference. The alarmists would have us believe that the fund is not a separate en-
tity, simply because its surplus is invested in U.S. government bonds. This
assertion contradicts the entire history of the system, as well as the law itself.
Since 1935, taxpayers have paid specially designated payroll taxes and received their benefits from these same funds.

What does it mean, then, to say that Social Security must be cut rather
than that the government must meet its obligations to the trust fund? When
the government bonds held by Bill Gates or Ross Perot or any other wealthy
individual or pension fund mature, nobody proposes that the creditors should
not be paid their principal. Yet the reformers insist that the 144 million Americans who loan money to the U.S. Treasury from the Social Security trust
fund somehow do not have the same claim. One reason they are able to get
away with this assertion is that the Treasury's current borrowing from the
trust fund is not counted as part of the federal unified budget deficit. Thus,
the budget was considered in surplus in 1998 when government borrowing
from other sources was reduced to less than zero, even though it was still
borrowing $100 billion from Social Security. If not for this accounting con-
vention, we would have had an approximately $31 billion budget deficit.

In 1999 the annual surplus, excluding interest, of the Social Security trust
fund was projected to reach its peak. From that point, the annual amount that
the Treasury can borrow from the trust fund falls, and it is at this point that
Social Security begins to "add to" the federal budget deficit. But this is merely
an accounting convention: in reality, the federal government will simply begin to replace some of the money that it had previously borrowed from the
trust fund with money borrowed from other sources. Since the borrowing
from Social Security was not counted as part of the budget deficit, but the
borrowing that replaces it *is* counted, the budget deficit grows.

Demography as Destiny

In an era in which each passing month sees another social problem or
phenomenon—beauty, crime, mental illness, obesity, adultery, divorce—proclaimed to be a product of biological evolution, economics has been relatively

---

surplus to the federal government rather than having invested it in private stocks or bonds
should not be used to make Social Security beneficiaries pay, in the form of reduced benefits,
for any fiscal tightening that may be applied to the rest of the budget.

Social Security and Its Critics

lucky to preserve its character as a social, rather than a natural, science, in spite of the self-imposed irrelevance or antisocial biases of its high theory. However fantastic the assumptions of its microfoundations, or truncated its conception of society as a collection of individual specimens of Homo economicus interacting through market transactions, economics has at least continued to seek social, and not biological, explanations for the phenomena under its purview. That being the case in the realm of theory, the policy arena is easily diverted by intellectual fads. So we should not be surprised at the receptive audience, inundated as it is with late-twentieth-century biodeter–minism, that can be found for an argument that derives a large part of our macroeconomic future from demographic trends. Everyone knows that there was a big spike in the birthrate beginning about 50 years ago that created what is called the baby boom generation. Countless feature stories in the popular media have tracked how the aging of the baby boomers has influenced every-thing from congressional elections to classic-rock radio stations around the country. If one generation is large enough to exert such a profound influence over our politics and culture, it is only natural to believe, especially if the story is repeated enough, that this cohort's retirement will hit the economy like an asteroid crashing into Earth.

One's suspicions might be aroused by the fact that we fed, clothed, housed, and educated all these people when they were dependents and still managed to invest enough to create the most rapid period of growth in American eco-nomic history. If we could take care of these people when they were young, why should it place an intolerable strain on our economy to provide for their retirement[2]—especially when that economy is going to be three to four times the size of the one that sustained the baby boomers until they were ready to enter the labor force?

The doomsayers have selectively used a raft of statistics to buttress their case.[3] For example, we are often told that the population of senior citizens (over 65) is expected to double by 2030, from 35.2 million today to 68.4 mil-lion. However, the rate of increase over the last 33 years was not that differ-ent: we went from 18.5 million senior citizens in 1965 to 35.2 million in 1999. These numbers by themselves do not mean very much. For example, if the

---

2. Richard Leone 1997 has emphasized this point.

3. For an example of this selective presentation, as well as the use of other devices discussed in this chapter, see Urban Institute 1998.

elderly were 1 percent of the population, then even if they doubled in percentage terms to 2 percent, no one would be worried. In fact, the proportion of people over 65 is 12.7 percent today and will grow to 20 percent by 2030. At the same time, the economy is projected to grow by 59 percent. Can an economy that is 59 percent bigger support an increase of this size in its retired population? There is little reason to doubt that it can, and, as we will see, with little adverse impact on the rising living standards of the rest of the nation.

Another statistic played up by the reformers is the ratio of workers to retirees. It is often noted, for example, that the number of workers paying Social Security taxes for every retiree drawing benefits will fall from 3.3 today to 2.1 by the year 2030 (SSA 1999, table II.F19). It is thus argued that the system will become unsustainable without serious benefit cuts. But the decline in this ratio has actually been considerably steeper in the past. In 1955 there were 8.6 workers per retiree, and the decline from 8.6 to 3.3 did not precipitate any economic disaster.

These figures also neglect to take into account the reduced costs faced by the working population from having a smaller proportion of children to support. A more accurate measure of the actual burden faced by the employed labor force would be the total dependency ratio, which includes both retirees and children relative to the number of workers. This ratio is projected to increase from 0.708 today to 0.796 in 2035 (SSA 1999, table II.H1). This is not a huge increase, and the latter figure is considerably below the ratio for the year 1965, which was 0.947. Thus, it seems that, in comparison to the past, the increase in the future burden of caring for a larger elderly population will be offset to a large extent by the reduced costs of education, child care, and other expenses of caring for dependent children (SSA 1999, table II.H1).

But even without taking into account the reduction in costs associated with the smaller number of children in the future, the figures on the number of elderly and the ratio of workers to retirees are misleading because they are taken so drastically out of context. To say that Social Security will go broke because of the declining number of workers per retiree is like saying that we should be very hungry right now because the percentage of the workforce in agriculture has declined from 5.1 to 1.1 over the last 40 years. The problem is that simple dependency ratios do not take into account productivity increases. Just as we can now feed the nation and in fact export a large agricultural surplus with vastly fewer people employed in agriculture, it is also true that fewer workers can support a larger number of retirees as the productivity of the entire economy grows.

This example illustrates how meaningless it is to cite scary-looking demographic or labor force statistics in isolation. In order to project the state of Social Security's financing in the future, it is necessary to take into account all of the variables that affect both revenue and payouts, including the aging of the population, the rate of growth of the labor force and wages (the latter are related to productivity growth), projected rates of unemployment, and interest rates. The Social Security actuaries have incorporated these trends, and the results are, as noted above, quite reassuring. Since the reformers are not willing (or able) to make the case that the trustees' intermediate assumptions are overly optimistic, they cannot challenge the results—and they do not. But that does not prevent a lot of people who, for various reasons, would like to create the impression that Social Security faces serious problems from focusing on whatever portions of the overall picture will make their case appear plausible.

Unfunded Liabilities, Ponzi Schemes, and Other Rhetorical Devices

Social Security's detractors have a few other tricks they like to throw into the mix in order to create the impression that the whole system is some kind of a scam. One of these is the concept of "unfunded liabilities." The argument is based on a view of Social Security that likens it to a private pension system. With this model in hand, Peter Peterson warns us that "the federal government has already promised to today's adults $8 trillion in future Social Security benefits beyond the value of the taxes they have paid to date." On this basis he concludes that the system has $8 trillion in "unfunded liabilities" (Peterson 1996, 44). This is a big number, and it is quite meaningless. Social Security is not a private pension system. Private pension systems do not have the power to collect a payroll tax from 144 million employees and their employers. As noted above, retirees who are receiving Social Security benefits this year are paid from the contributions of workers who are currently employed (and their employers); for the next 30 years, these payroll taxes will amount to an average of more than $550 billion per year. The fact that the system is currently taking in more than it pays out, and is accumulating a surplus in anticipation of the increase in payouts as the baby boomers retire, does not alter the system's basic "pay-as-you-go" financing. In such a system, it makes no sense to compare the program's committed payouts to money already collected in the past. All that matters is the balance between future revenues (including the accumulated assets of the trust fund and its returns) and future payouts. And on that score, the program is secure for the foreseeable future.

As will be explained in chapter 7, there is little economic reason to favor a fully funded system over a pay-as-you-go setup, since there is no reason to believe that national savings would be any higher under a fully funded system. Part of the hostility toward a pay-as-you-go system results from the fact that this is one of the few ways that income can be redistributed from the current generation of workers to their elders. The Social Security system was designed to do just that, on the idea that each generation has a higher standard of living, on average, than its predecessor. And that higher standard of living is based on the sacrifices of previous generations, which helped to build the capital stock and infrastructure that enable current generations to enjoy the benefits of the resulting gains in productivity. For those who are against the redistribution of income as a matter of principle, pay-as-you-go is difficult to swallow.

Some of the program's most vocal critics have therefore attacked Social Security as a "Ponzi scheme," that is, a pyramid scheme in which the first participants benefit at the expense of those who join in after them, with the whole structure collapsing underneath the hapless Generation X or perhaps their progeny. Exhibit A in this argument is the declining rate of return on Social Security contributions. For example, an average-income, single, male employee born in 1920 would have received an expected real return of 2.73 percent on his contributions, as opposed to 1.37 percent for someone born in 1943.

It is indeed true that in a pay-as-you-go system the rate of return will decline from the time the system is initiated until it reaches maturity. The program was signed into law in August 1935, and the first beneficiaries, who began to receive benefits in 1945, had paid into the system for only a short time. It was not until the late 1970s that the first cohorts of workers who had paid into the system for their whole working lives began to retire; in the meantime, the total number of retirement beneficiaries drawing benefits has grown from 1.3 million in 1945 to 37.9 million in 1998 (SSA 1999, table II.H2). As a result of these dynamics, the payroll tax has been steadily increased: from 1.0 percent in 1936 to 6.2 percent on both the employee and the employer today. In 1983 benefits were also cut significantly by raising the retirement age to 67 (phased in for retirees beginning in the year 2000).

There is nothing particularly sinister about the declining rate of return generated by the arithmetic of a pay-as-you-go system. The alternative in 1935 would have been to postpone the initiation of Social Security for a few generations until a collective pension fund could have been built up, with payments based on the returns generated from these assets. This was not an attractive option in the middle of the Great Depression, when so many senior citizens, as well as their families, were impoverished. The nation opted instead for a pact between generations, and this accord has been maintained. Is it unfair that earlier recipients received a higher return for their contributions? Perhaps some will see it that way, but how many Generation X-ers would trade their grandparents' return on Social Security taxes *and also* their lifetime income for their own? This is what really matters: not that the rate of return on each individual's payroll taxes is equal across all generations, but that no particular cohort has to make inordinate sacrifices with regard to their standard of living. There is no plausible scenario under which the obligations of the Social Security system could cause this to happen to future generations. (This argument is explained more thoroughly in chapter 2.)

Advocates of privatization have recently crafted appeals based on the idea that various demographic groups could earn a better return from a privatized account. Their arguments are based on a number of flawed assumptions, such as exaggerated estimates of the rate of return that people could earn in the stock market (see chapter 5). However, there is one particular appeal that has entered the discussion only recently: the argument that African Americans get a much lower return than whites from Social Security and would therefore be better off with a privatized alternative. The Heritage Foundation, in a report that received a fair amount of attention in the press (Stevenson 1998d), has made this claim (Beach and Davis 1998).

Because of the large difference in life expectancy between African American and white men,[4] African American men get a much lower return than their white counterparts in terms of retirement benefits. In fact, there are similar differences in life expectancy by income and occupation irrespective of race (Rogot, Sorlie, and Johnson 1992). But the Social Security system also provides benefits to survivors of deceased workers and to disabled workers, and about 25 percent of the children who receive survivor benefits and about 18 percent of the recipients of disability awards are black. Since African Ameri-

---

4. Past and projected life expectancies are from the National Center for Health Statistics and the Office of the Actuary, Social Security Administration.

cans compose about 12 percent of the population, their claim on survivor and disability benefits compensates for at least part, if not all, of the reduced retirement benefits they get from Social Security.

The calculation that African Americans would get a higher return from privatized accounts not only excludes the survivor and disability portions of the system, but also the transition costs that would be necessary in any switch to a privatized system. Today's Social Security beneficiaries are paid from current payroll taxes. Diverting these payroll taxes into private accounts would require a wait of 40 years before a retiree could draw benefits from the principal. In the meantime, retired workers would still have to be paid. Thus, for several decades employees would have to pay two sets of taxes: their mandatory contributions to private retirement accounts, plus the taxes necessary to support all those who are already drawing benefits. These transition taxes are significant: under the main partial privatization plan advanced by a faction of the 1997 Advisory Council on Social Security, transition costs were estimated at 1.52 percent of payroll, spread out over the next 72 years. And that plan proposed to divert only about half of Social Security payroll taxes into "personal security accounts" (PSAs). If we add the transition taxes into the calculation, it can no longer be asserted that African American men, or any other demographic group, would fare better under a privatized system—in fact, their returns would be negative for the next few generations.

Although privatization would only worsen the situation, the enormous disparity in retirement years across racial and class lines raises profound issues of public health in the United States. Social Security alone cannot resolve these problems; they will have to be addressed through other policies such as national health insurance, occupational health measures, and, perhaps most important, efforts to reduce poverty and income inequality. To the extent that the Social Security system can be made more progressive in its tax and benefit structure, it could in the meantime provide some counterbalance to these disparities in years of retirement. Ironically, almost all advocates of Social Security reform—including those who favor privatization—want to raise the retirement age, a step that would greatly aggravate racial disparities in the system based on life expectancy (see chapter 6).

In sum, there is no "demographic tidal wave" that will drown Social Security's finances in the ensuing decades. The baby boomers' retirement has already been taken into account, and there is no need for further benefit cuts. And there is no pyramid scheme or diversion of Social Security's revenues to other purposes. Any shortfall that might occur 30 or 40 years down the road will be easily handled by a population that has much greater income than we have today. Any assertion to the contrary is false and misleading and can be supported only by taking selected demographic and economic projections out of context, or through other sleights of hand.

2 | Generating Phony Wars with Generational Accounting

THE MAIN THRUST of the attack against Social Security centers on the notion of intergenerational unfairness. The argument goes like this: Social Security was a great deal for our grandparents and parents, but their good fortune comes at the expense of current and future generations of workers, who are going to get stuck with a huge tax burden. A number of organizations targeted at the young have been created precisely to promote this sort of argument against Social Security and other benefits for the elderly, and politicians and pundits have been anxious to embrace their cause.

This argument of generational inequity also appears in a more sophisticated form in a system called "generational accounting." Developed by three prominent economists—Alan Auerbach, a professor at the University of California, Berkeley; Jagadeesh Gokhale, an economist at the Federal Reserve Bank of Cleveland; and Laurence Kotlikoff, a professor at Boston University—generational accounting centers on the calculation of a "lifetime net tax rate." It has generally shown that successive age cohorts will face higher and higher lifetime tax burdens, to the point where 80, 90, or even 100 percent of their incomes will be eaten up by taxes. The future looks bleak indeed.

At its peak, generational accounting achieved a significant degree of acceptance within the economics profession, with articles appearing in some of the economics profession's leading journals. On the policy side, the Office of Management and Budget included a set of generational accounts in its official analyses of the budget for several years in the early 1990s, and the Congressional Budget Office considered adopting the system as an official budgeting procedure. Generational accounts have also been constructed for Norway, Italy, New Zealand, and many other countries.[1]

At the simplest level, the argument of generational inequity has some merit. Social Security was clearly a better deal for the first generations of recipients, who, because the pool of workers was large relative to the number of retirees being supported, paid relatively low rates of taxes into the system for only a portion of their working lives. However, as the size of the pool of workers has contracted relative to the number of retirees, it has been necessary to raise the tax rate to keep the system solvent, and further tax increases will be needed in the future if scheduled benefits are to be maintained. But tax rates can't keep rising forever. Is Social Security a Ponzi scheme? An unusual form of child abuse? The issue needs closer examination.

How Generational Accounting Works

Generational accounting is intended to provide a measure of the lifetime net tax burden that will be faced by people who are born at different points in time. In other words, it attempts to calculate the average amount of taxes that a person born in a particular year will pay over his or her lifetime. The tax burden is calculated as a "net tax" in that it includes all the taxes that a person pays out over a lifetime, less benefits such as Social Security or Medicare that a typical person receives. This net tax is then expressed as a percentage of projected lifetime income to get the net tax burden for each age cohort.

These calculations project immense tax burdens for today's young and for generations yet to be born. According to a set of generational accounts that appeared in the President's *Analysis of the Budget* (OMB 1994), the net tax burden for someone born in 1900 was just 23.6 percent. It rises to 30.6 percent for a person born in 1930, to 33.2 percent for someone born in 1950, and to 36.3 percent for a Generation X-er born in 1970. But the worst is yet to come: the generational accounting projects that the average net tax rate for all generations yet to be born will be 82.0 percent. This dire projection is based on the assumptions that the government's spending patterns will not change

---

1. The principles of generational accounting are set out in Auerbach, Gokhale, and Kotlikoff 1991. Kotlikoff 1993 presents the principles of generational accounting for a general audience. For analysis of the merits of generational accounting, see Haveman 1994 (with response from Kotlikoff), Cutler 1994, CBO 1995, and Goode and Steurele 1994. Examples of generational accounts can be found in the *Analytic Perspectives* that are published along with the official budget for the fiscal years 1993–95 (OMB 1992–94).

and that everyone currently alive receives all the benefits and pays no taxes higher than specified under current law.

How Generational Accounting Cooks the Books

Before panicking, it is worth examining how this horror story is constructed. It turns out that the numbers that appear in the generational accounts depend a great deal on some of the assumptions that are used to construct the accounts, and altering these assumptions in reasonable ways gives very different results. Three assumptions are key: (1) the discount rate used in the accounts, (2) the treatment of education spending, and (3) the projected rate of growth of health care costs. Replacing the numbers used in the generational accounts with reasonable alternatives causes the nightmare scenario to vanish.

Discounting Our Children's Futures

The first assumption—the discount rate used in constructing the accounts—is a bit technical, but it is important to the result. The discount rate is the interest rate we use to compare income and tax payments at different points in time. Money earns interest, and so money is worth more in the future if the interest rate is higher than the inflation rate. (In this discussion we will assume that inflation is zero, so that prices never change. In this scenario the real interest rate—the interest rate received after adjusting for inflation—is exactly the same as the nominal interest rate.) So, for example, if I have $1,000 today and can get 5.0 percent interest, I will have $1,050 next year if I lend out my money. Put another way, having $1,000 this year is the same to me as having $1,050 next year.

It is standard for economists to use discount rates like this to take into account the possibility that money can be lent out and earn interest through time. The discount rate selected for a particular analysis can make a big difference, especially over a long period. For example, at a 2.0 percent discount rate, having $1,000 in the bank 60 years from now would be the same as having $305 today; at a 6.0 percent discount rate that same $1,000 is equivalent to just $30 today.[2]

In the standard version of generational accounts, analysts use a 6.0 percent real discount rate to compare flows of taxes, benefits, and earnings at

2. This is calculated by taking 1.06 to the 60th power ($1.06^{60} = 33.0$) and then dividing it into $1,000 ($1,000 / 33.0 = $30.30).

different points in time.[3] This rate is much higher than the 2.0 percent conventionally used in analyses of Social Security (see, e.g., Steuerle and Bakija 1994; Wolff and Chernick 1996), and it has the effect of raising the net tax burden enormously for future generations because it lowers the value of the Social Security and Medicare benefits that future generations are projected to receive during their long retirements. Simply changing the discount rate from 6.0 percent to 3.0 percent lowers the lifetime net tax burden for future generations by 29–39 percentage points.[4] Using the standard 2.0 percent rate lowers the net tax burden an additional 11.6 percentage points, to less than 40 percent.[5] This accounting shift alone should let today's youth breathe a lot easier.

There is no easy answer as to which is the correct discount rate for assessing tax and benefit flows over time. However, certain anomalies arise if the discount rate used in these sorts of calculations exceeds the economy's rate of growth. The most important anomaly is that the discounted value of future income eventually goes to zero. For example, with a 6.0 percent discount rate, the value of the nation's projected output in the year 2699 is just $1.62. By this assessment, a measure that might raise the nation's income by $100 this year but end the world after 2700, when its total output would be worth about zero, would be a good policy, according to the generational accountants. If we think it is unreasonable to apply a discount rate that implies ending the world at some point in the future, then we should never use a discount rate greater than the economy's rate of growth for the sort of long-term calculations that appear in the generational accounts. Moreover, as noted above, the lower discount rate goes far toward eliminating the horror story the generational accountants have constructed.

3. Generational accounts have also been calculated with 2.0 percent, 3.0 percent, and 9.0 percent discount rates, but the accounts featured most prominently by proponents of generational accounting, and in official documents, have used a 6.0 percent rate.

4. The reduction of 29 percentage points appears in a set of calculations performed by the Congressional Budget Office, which used a computer program and data provided by Auerbach, Gokhale, and Kotlikoff (CBO 1995, 30). The reduction of 39 percentage points was obtained using a model that loosely follows the one described in Auerbach, Gokhale, and Kotlikoff 1991 and appears in Baker 1995, 19. The net lifetime tax burden for future generations is 79.0 percentage points in the CBO model and 89.0 percentage points in Baker 1995. Some of this difference is attributable to differences in the way the models were constructed, and some reflects different budget assumptions.

5. This calculation can be found in Baker 1995, 19.

Will Education Really Impoverish Our Children?

The treatment of education in the generational accounts also provides a basis for false fears. While most of us might think that education spending helps our children, the generational accounts don't quite see it this way. In the standard versions of the accountants, education spending is treated just like any other expense, paid for with tax revenues levied against our children.[6] In other words, the more we spend on our children, the worse off they are.

Education is the largest single expenditure category when all levels of government (federal, state, and local) are combined. In the 1993–94 fiscal year, the last year for which all the data are available, the various levels of government spent a combined total of $353.3 billion, or more than 5 percent of the gross domestic product (GDP), to educate the nation's youth (*ERP* 1998, table B-86). This money should help future generations of workers to be more productive on the job and also enhance their lives off the job. To keep a consistent set of accounts by age cohort, it might seem appropriate that the education expenditures on the young be treated as a benefit to the young, just as Medicare expenditures on the elderly are treated as a benefit to the elderly. (In generational accounting, benefits are treated as a negative tax; therefore, treating education expenditures as a benefit would decrease the lifetime net tax burden of today's young and the generations to come.)

Treating education expenditures in this manner makes a big difference in the accounts. In a set of generational accounts modeled after the standard version developed by Auerbach, Gokhale, and Kotlikoff (1991), counting education as a benefit reduced the net lifetime tax rate for future generations by 31.7 percentage points, more than one-third of the total burden (Baker 1995, 21–22). This simple and completely defensible change in procedures goes a long way toward eliminating the nightmare that the generational accounts project for our grandchildren.

One reason that the impact of counting education spending as a benefit is so large has to do with the 6.0 percent discount rate used in the generational

---

6. Some generational accounts calculate education as a benefit to children (e.g., Auerbach et al. 1993). Auerbach, Gokhale, and Kotlikoff acknowledge that this is the correct way to treat education spending (1991, 72), but in most of their accounts they do not differentiate spending on education from any other form of government expenditure.

accounts. Since education is a benefit received early in life, before any taxes are paid, its value compounds greatly with a high discount rate. At lower rates, the treatment of education spending makes less of a difference—but at lower discount rates the future horror is greatly alleviated to begin with.

If Health Care Costs Destroy the Economy, What Will Happen to Tax Rates?

The third questionable assumption built into the generational accounts is the growth rate of health care costs. The projections in the generational accounts for public sector health care spending, especially for Medicare and Medicaid, show expenditures growing at a rapid rate. Measured as a share of GDP, these programs are projected to more than double by 2030: Medicare from 3 percent of GDP in 1995 to 8 percent in 2030, and Medicaid from 1 percent in 1995 to 3 percent in 2030 (CBO 1996, 80). (Approximately 60 percent of Medicaid expenditures provide health care for people over age 65.) State expenditures on Medicaid roughly match federal expenditures and would thus rise by approximately the same amount.

Part of the growth in these programs is attributable to the aging of the population, the demographic threat noted by the generational accountants. But the aging of the population accounts for only one-third of the projected increase in the cost of publicly provided health care over this period. The other two-thirds of the increase is the result of projections of rapid growth in health care costs more generally, in both public and private sectors.

Health care costs in the public and private sectors have always moved together in the United States. Although short periods of divergence have occurred (on a per capita basis, public sector costs grew more slowly in the 1980s, whereas private sector costs grew more slowly in the 1990s), over any long period the growth rates are quite close. If we assume the same growth rate of per capita private sector health care costs as the accounts assume for the public sector, then private sector health care costs will bankrupt the economy. By the year 2030, the median family will be paying more than 20 percent of its income for its health insurance premiums, co-payments, and out-of-pocket health care expenditures (Baker 1998).[7] If this projection proves

---

7. This figure is obtained by taking the difference between the after-tax, after-health-care family incomes in scenarios I and III in Baker 1998, subtracting the difference between the after-tax incomes in the two scenarios, and adding the base level projections for health care that appear in Baker's appendix table 1.

accurate, then most families will either have to do without regular access to health care or impoverish themselves in their efforts to pay the bills. In this scenario, Medicare and Medicaid will be a real burden on taxpayers, as the generational accountants warn. But this focus seems somewhat backward. Even if Medicare and Medicaid are eliminated altogether, families will face an enormous burden from health care costs if expenses follow their projected course. The message one might derive from these projections is the urgent need to curb costs in the nation's health care system. The generational accounts conceal this problem by focusing exclusively on the public sector.

Removing the scenario of exploding health care costs goes far toward eliminating the fiscal nightmare projected in the accounts. A set of accounts that have Medicare and Medicaid costs rising in step with per capita income, overall inflation, and the aging of the population would show a net lifetime tax burden for future generations 29.4 percentage points lower than in the accounts based on exploding health care costs (Baker 1995, 25).

What the Recount Shows

The generational accounts that have appeared in the president's *Analytic Perspectives* on the budget and received so much attention from politicians and the media have shown that future generations will face net lifetime tax burdens of 80–90 percent. However, once some of the dubious assumptions or methodological procedures are adjusted, a different picture emerges, as shown in table 2-1. The projected lifetime net tax rate falls from over 80 percent to a bit over 20 percent. In other words, the nightmare scenario coming out of the generational accounts is nothing more than a scare story. Once reasonable assumptions and accounting procedures are employed, it becomes clear that future generations have little to fear from exorbitant tax burdens. Health care costs indeed pose a serious problem, but the solution lies not in adjustments to Medicare and Medicaid but in national policies to restructure the entire national health care system.

The treatment of health care is only a small part of a phony score card on the topic of generational equity. The real trick performed by the generational accountants is to set up a bogus criterion of generational equity. According to the generational accountants, generational equity is achieved if all generations face the same lifetime net tax rate. It is a safe bet that no one will ever want to pay higher taxes, but a low tax rate is not ordinarily accepted as the exclusive criterion of well-being. For example, few people would want to claim

Table 2-1. Lifetime Net Tax Burden Projected by Generational Accounts Under Different Assumptions

Discount rate	Standard account	No excessive health inflation	Counting education as a transfer	No excessive health inflation and counting education as a transfer
2%	37.4	32.5	27.2	22.9
3%	49	38.6	35.2	24.4
6%	88.7	59.3	57	16.8
9%	166.2	107.6	102	−10.6

Source: Baker 1995.

that Bill Gates's high tax rate makes him worse off than an unemployed factory worker. Rather, our view of people's well-being usually depends on their overall standard of living. The tax rate affects this standard, but it is a small part of the whole picture. Furthermore, when taxes are increased to provide a public service that we value, such as parks or roads, we probably wouldn't view such taxes as an unfair burden.

Moreover, the government can burden its citizens in other ways than through taxes. A good example is the military draft. From 1940 until 1972 men in the United States faced the prospect of having to devote two or more years of their lives to military service, a tremendous sacrifice in terms of postponed education and careers, not to mention the risk to life and limb. Yet there is no entry for the draft in the generational accounts, and partly as a result of this omission they show the generations born after World War II doing worse than their parents, who had to fight that war. (After all, their parents are getting a better deal on Social Security.) Clearly, a system of accounting that could reach this conclusion has serious problems as a measure of generational equity.

Another major failing of the generational accounts is that they treat all government expenditures as being of equal value in providing benefits to the generation that makes them. This system is problematic for two reasons. First, there are many types of government expenditure that are really investments, not consumption. For example, the government's current spending on constructing highways, mass transit systems, airports, and research and development will yield far more benefits in the future than it will over the next few years. But the generational accounts do not differentiate government investment from government consumption, creating a situation in which current

generations actually appear to be imposing a greater burden on future generations if they undertake expenditures to improve the physical infrastructure or
the state of scientific knowledge but borrow to finance part of the costs. Second, some government expenditures actually provide no direct benefit to the
generation that makes them. A good example is military spending. In principle, this spending may be necessary to protect the nation from foreign threats,
but it does not improve the material well-being of the population at the point
at which it is being carried through. This point is important in terms of the
generational accounts, because in previous years a far higher portion of the
nation's output was devoted to supporting the military. Through the Cold
War years from 1950 to 1989, military spending averaged 7.7 percent of GDP;
it exceeded 10 percent in peak years, such as during the Korean War. At present,
the military budget is approximately 3.4 percent of GDP (*ERP* 1998, table B-
74) and is projected to fall below 2.7 percent in the next 10 years.[8] The resources freed up by this decline will be available to meet other needs of the
population; in dollar terms, this difference translates into an additional $379
billion that the government has available to meet the needs of the population
in 1999. If in the future the country continues to be able to meet its defense
needs with a much smaller relative commitment of resources than in the Cold
War years, then future generations will benefit enormously. This point is altogether overlooked in the methodology in the generational accounts.

One last issue that needs to be considered before turning to some alternative projections of future living standards is the fact that the government passes
on more than debt to future generations; it also passes on assets. The generational accountants focus only on the debt side of the ledger: any action that
raises the debt creates a higher burden on future generations, and any action
that lowers the debt reduces the burden. This can lead to some perverse book-
keeping. Building infrastructure like roads or communications systems is worth
nothing in the generational accounts. But if the government were to sell off
all its assets, such as national parks and oil reserves, the generational accounts
would show a benefit for future generations. Presenting our children and
grandchildren with a treeless, strip-mined, environmentally devastated country
appears to be a plus in the generational accounts.[9]

---

8. The Congressional Budget Office (1998) projects that in 2008 military spending
will be $357 billion (p. 64) and GDP will be $13,280 billion.

9. It is worth noting that the government can require payments that are not actually

In short, the generational accounts are inadequate as a means to inform us about the well-being of generations across time, and their narrow focus precludes them from providing us with a measure of the extent to which the government places a burden on households. The government has the responsibility of establishing and maintaining a physical, social, and natural environment in which we earn our livelihood and live our lives. The extent to which the government performs this task effectively and efficiently cannot be measured by the country's rate of taxation. Moreover, the tax burden is even more inappropriate as a measure of generational equity. Given all the inadequacies noted above, using generational accounting as a means to assess generational equity makes as much sense as using a bathroom scale to determine the quality of a painting.

How Will Our Children Really Fare?

While income is not a comprehensive measure of a person's well-being, it is reasonable to ask what sort of living standards future generations will be able to enjoy. The generational accountants are correct in pointing out that a larger share of before-tax income in the future will be required to support the retired population. But the question that needs to be answered is, what will happen to after-tax income in the years to come?

A recent analysis of current projections (Baker 1998) shows that demographic trends actually provide little basis for fear for future generations. Real wages, on average, should continue to increase at a moderate pace throughout the next century, and the projected growth rate in wages will be far faster than the growth in the tax burden that is attributable to the needs of a larger population of retirees. In short, the after-tax income of our children and grandchildren should be far higher than the levels people today enjoy.

However, there are grounds for concern about the future that have nothing to do with demographics. As discussed above, projected rates of growth in health care costs pose potential problems, not just in terms of taxes needed to sustain Medicare and Medicaid but in terms of private sector spending as well.

The other basis for concern in projections for future income is the recent

---

taxes. For example, the Clinton administration's health care proposal required that individuals have private insurance (either provided through their employer or purchased directly). This payment would not have been treated as a tax in the generational accounts. Similarly, government-mandated savings, in place of payments to Social Security, would not be treated as taxes in the generational accounts.

trend of increasing wage inequality. Over the last two decades a large redistribution of the rewards from work has occurred from lower-wage to higher-wage workers. As a result, the real wage of the typical worker actually fell by 5.5 percent from 1979 to 1997 (Mishel, Bernstein, and Schmitt 1999, 131). While the highest-paid workers have seen gains over this period, the bulk of the workforce has experienced declining real wages. In the last few years, the redistribution from low-wage to high-wage workers has been compounded by a redistribution from wage income generally to profit income. The share of income in the corporate sector that goes to capital income (profits plus interest) rose from 18.4 percent in 1989 to 21.7 percent in 1997.[10] This redistribution from labor to capital lowered wages by an additional 4.0 percent for an average worker. If this upward redistribution continues into the future, then most of the population will experience little improvement in living standards in coming years, while those at the top will do quite well.

If projections of exploding health care costs prove accurate and current trends in inequality continue, then our children and grandchildren will have much to worry about. Health care costs will be soaring at a time when most families will be seeing little or no increase in their before-tax income. However, changing demographics will be the least of their problems. This picture deserves a closer examination.

Rising Incomes, Changing Demographics

The most important point to keep in mind when we consider long-term projections about the future is that, thanks to productivity growth, living standards generally rise through time. Productivity growth means that each worker can produce more goods and services in the same amount of time. It can occur because workers have more or better capital (machines, computers, communications equipment) to work with, because workers are better educated and trained, or because work is better organized. Economists dispute exactly how much each of these factors has contributed to productivity growth, but clearly all have played a role.

---

10. According to data in the National Income and Product Accounts, in 1989 domestic corporate income was $2,580.7 billion, profits with inventory valuation adjustment and capital consumption adjustment were $322 billion, and net interest was $152.7 billion. In 1997 domestic corporate income was $3,990 billion, profits with inventory valuation adjustment and capital consumption adjustment were $704.2 billion, and net interest was $157.8 billion.

Productivity growth—sometimes very rapid growth—is a regular feature of market economies. In Japan the annual rate of productivity growth from 1973 to 1995 was 3.1 percent (Schmitt and Mishel 1998). The average annual rate of productivity growth in the United States from 1947 to 1973 was 2.5 percent (*ERP* 1998, table B-47), but since then it has slowed considerably, averaging just 1.1 percent annually. No one knows exactly why the rate of productivity growth has dropped so much from the early postwar period, or if the current slow rate of productivity growth is likely to continue.[11] But even this slow rate of growth provides a basis for rising living standards through time.

The projections for future income in this section follow the assumption of the trustees of the Social Security fund that the low productivity growth of the last 25 years will largely continue into the future. A 1.1 percent rate of annual productivity growth, sustained over 35 years, will allow for a 46.7 percent improvement in living standards. Over 55 years, it will allow for an improvement in living standards of more than 80.0 percent. Even this is a relatively pessimistic picture, and it would be much brighter if productivity growth rebounded somewhat, say to 2.0 percent annually. In this case, living standards would double in 35 years and triple in 55 years. For the sake of consistency, though, this analysis uses the 1.1 percent rate employed by the trustees.[12]

The Base Case

The base case in these projections assumes that taxes are increased as needed to support the projected demographic changes in the population. It also allocates the specific taxes to the income groups that are expected to bear them. For example, the projected decline in the portion of the population that is enrolled in schools should lead to a decline in the state and local taxes used to support public schools. These taxes, such as sales taxes and excise taxes, fall disproportionately on low- and moderate-income families, so a reduction in state and local taxes should disproportionately benefit these groups. At the federal level, these projections assume that Medicare continues to be funded

11. There is nothing inevitable about slower rates of productivity growth. Several European countries, such as France, Germany, and Belgium, which have levels of productivity that are comparable to those in the United States, continue to enjoy rates of productivity growth that are close to 2.0 percent annually. So there is no reason to believe that the United States cannot in principle also attain these higher productivity growth rates.

12. These projections are explained more fully in Baker 1998.

partially out of payroll taxes and partially out of general revenue[13] and that the Social Security fund continues to be financed through the payroll tax.

This last point deserves some clarification. At present, the Social Security trust fund is building up an enormous surplus (projected to reach about $2 trillion by 2010) to help cover the cost of the retirement of the baby boom generation. The surplus is kept in the form of government bonds, which the Treasury Department sells to the Social Security fund. These bonds pay the same rate of interest as other government bonds that are issued at the same time. As the baby boom generation begins to retire it will be necessary to draw down this surplus to pay out all the benefits that have been promised. This analysis assumes that the fund redeems its bonds and that the government pays back the borrowed money out of general revenue, not through an increase in the payroll tax. This distinction is important because the payroll tax is an extremely regressive tax. Most of the government's general revenue is raised through individual and corporate income taxes, both of which are progressive. The regressiveness of the payroll tax can be justified in the context of Social Security's progressive payback structure, but it cannot be justified as a means to fund government operations in general. Failing to pay back the bonds held by the Social Security trust fund out of general revenue would effectively mean that the government had used the Social Security payroll tax, its most regressive tax, to finance other government programs. Alternatively, this method of payback could be seen as taxing workers twice for the same benefit. The surplus was originally built up through a designated Social Security tax, and if the government does not repay the bonds held by the trust fund, workers will then have to be taxed a second time to get benefits they have already paid for. In short, repaying the Social Security trust fund out of general revenue is a matter of both equity and honesty. This analysis assumes we follow such a course, that is, that the federal government does not default on the bonds held by the trust fund and repays them out of general revenue.

In the base case, the future looks pretty good. Figure 2-1 shows projections for the median family's after-tax income through 2070. For a family in the middle fifth of the income distribution, after-tax income should be ap-

13. At present, the Hospital Insurance portion of the program, Part A, is funded through the payroll tax. Three-quarters of the Supplemental Insurance portion, Part B, is financed through general revenue. The remaining quarter of the costs of this program are paid by Medicare beneficiaries in monthly premiums.

Generational Accounting

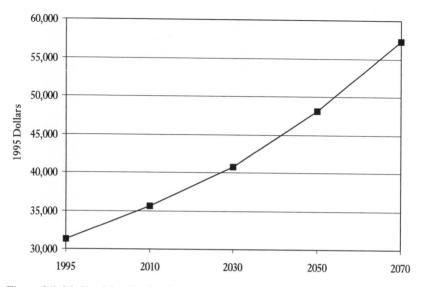

Figure 2-1. Median After-Tax Family Income: Base Case

proximately 30.0 percent higher in 2030 than it is today. These projections also assume a gradual increase (up to an extra eight days by 2030) in the amount of time off that workers receive each year. The projection shows that, under pessimistic assumptions about productivity growth, we can expect that a typical family will be able to cover the tax burden associated with the baby boomers' retirement and still have 30 percent more after-tax income and eight more days of vacation each year than today's typical family. This does not sound like a demographic catastrophe.

This methodology allows us to examine just how hard an impact changing demographics will have. The base case cited above already includes the negative impact on family income of the taxes needed to support an increasing elderly population. However, it is possible to construct a scenario that assumes that the demographic composition of the population does not change over the next 35 years; the difference between the level of after-tax income in the two scenarios measures the projected cost of demographic change. It is also possible to directly compare the impact of demographic change with the impact of excessive health care inflation and the continuation of current trends in wage inequality. These differences are illustrated in figure 2-2, which compares the impact of each of these trends on the projected after-tax, after-health-care income for a typical family in the year 2030. It is important to

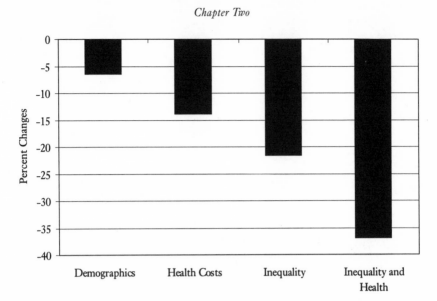

Figure 2-2. Impacts on After-Tax, After-Health Care Family Income, Year 2030

remember that the comparison is with the baseline shown in figure 2-1, where the typical family will have experienced a rise in real income of more than 30 percent by 2030. The first bar shows the reduction in after-tax, after-health-care family income that results from the demographic changes that are projected for 2030. The decline is a bit over 6.0 percent compared to a scenario in which there were no demographic changes. Much of this decline is due not to projected tax increases but rather to the fact that the current Social Security tax is approximately 2.0 percent higher than would be necessary if there were no demographic changes projected for the future. In other words, the Social Security tax could be cut by 2.0 percentage points tomorrow if we were not trying to build up a surplus to support the retirement of the baby boom generation. It is also worth noting that about half the projected increase in the ratio of retirees to workers over the next 35 years is attributable to increasing life expectancies, not the baby boomers' retirement. This "problem" of greater longevity will get worse as each generation comes to enjoy longer life spans.

Regardless of whether one views the projected impact of demographic changes as large or small, the projected impacts of health care inflation and wage inequality are clearly much larger. The second bar shows that the projected decline in after-tax, after-healthcare family income due to excessive growth in health care costs will be nearly 14 percent, more than twice as large as the decline attributable to demographic changes.[14] If recent trends in inequality continue into the future, the impact on a typical family will be even greater: a decline of nearly 22.0 percent in after-tax, after-health-care income compared to the baseline case. This decline is more than three time as large as the projected impact of demographic changes.

The combined impact of excessive health care inflation and a continuation of recent trends in inequality will be devastating for the typical family, lowering its income by nearly 37.0 percent compared with the baseline scenario. This impact is more than six times as large as the projected effect of demographic changes and larger than the projected increase in after-tax, after-health-care family income in the baseline scenario (see fig. 2-1). This means that if both current trends in health care costs and wage inequality continue through the first three decades of the twenty-first century, most families will actually be experiencing declining living standards over this period. Clearly these trends pose a far greater threat to the living standards of young and future generations of workers than does the aging of the population.

What the Real Generational Accounts Show

Through a combination of poor methodology and questionable assumptions, the technique known as generational accounting has provided a basis for scaring people about the prospects of future generations. Its projections of future tax burdens of 80–90 percent have served not to illuminate the discussion of generational equity but instead to create a sense of panic, a sense that drastic measures for government programs are required now to head off a major intergenerational theft. But a more careful, detailed analysis of future incomes and taxes reveals that there is little reason to doubt that the tradition of intergenerational progress, of parents leaving a better world to their children and grandchildren, will endure, even under a pessimistic economic scenario. This not to say that the future is unalterably bright—continued economic inequality and an uncontrolled health care system could still rob a future generation of its prosperity, and that generation might be justifiably miffed that its parents and grandparents let accounting legerdemain distract them from the real problem.

14. These projections assume that per capita health care expenditures in the private sector grow at the same rate as the Health Care Financing Administration has projected for per capita expenditures in Medicare over this period.

3 | Entitlements for the Elderly: Medicare "Reform"

AFTER SOCIAL SECURITY, Medicare is the second major social insurance program for the elderly, providing some 39 million senior and disabled citizens with health insurance. The coverage is a tremendous help to its beneficiaries but it could be much better. It does not cover, for example, the often bankrupting expenses of long-term care for the 6.5 million elderly who need it, nor does it pay for prescription drugs, eyeglasses, hearing aids, dental care, or most preventive care. It thus leaves the average senior citizen spending 21 percent of his or her income on health care. The poor fare even worse, with health care taking 30 percent of their income (Moon, Kuntz, and Pounder 1996). But it is not for its incomplete coverage that Medicare has fallen prey to the creative destruction of entitlement reformers. Rather, the program is widely regarded to be, like Social Security, "unsustainable" in its present form (see, e.g., *New Orleans Times-Picayune* 1998). Demographic change is once again portrayed as the relentless enemy that will drag everyone—elderly and nonelderly alike—over the cliff when the baby boomers retire.

Of course, the demographic problem is not the only one that gets attention. Multibillion dollar Medicare fraud, for example, can make a big splash in the news. The stories sometimes border on satire, as in the case of a home health care firm that tried to include the BMW driven by the owners' son in college as a cost of doing business. Other reports are more ghastly, as if from a horror film: a cardiologist who received kickbacks from a pacemaker manufacturer is alleged to have implanted the devices in patients who did not need them (Hilzenrath 1997).

But for policy analysts and many so-called reformers, the demographic time bomb is the real terror. They often lump Social Security and Medicare together, in an attempt to saddle the former, which is financially sound, with the problems of rising health care costs. The solutions put forth for Medicare are, as in the case of Social Security, a mixture of cuts and privatization, and here the reformers have made much more progress toward their goals.

In 1997 the Senate passed an increase in the age of eligibility from 65 to 67, a move that would have pushed more than 500,000 people aged 65 and 66 into the ranks of the uninsured (Waidman 1998). The same bill also provided for significant means testing in the form of steep premiums for upper-income seniors. It failed to clear the House but won much praise for its courage from policymakers and pundits. Meanwhile, the marketization of Medicare has proceeded steadily: the number of seniors receiving their Medicare coverage through health maintenance organizations has tripled over the last six years and now stands at 6 million (HCFA 1997a).

Are we really facing a demographic crisis in the provision of health care for the nation's elderly? And will the further corporatization and privatization of Medicare increase the productivity and efficiency of the health care system, thereby helping to bring its costs under control? The future of health care for Americans, and not only those over 65, may well depend on the answers to these questions.

There are two ways in which health care costs take a bite out of household income: through public spending, which shows up in a household's taxes, and through its own private spending. The latter can take the form of out-of-pocket expenses or the payment of insurance premiums. Even if the premium is paid partially or in full by the employer, economists tend to assume that employees absorb the employer's payment in the form of reduced wages.

In the United States the majority of heath care spending is still private, but not by much: the public sector, which includes Medicare and Medicaid, now accounts for about 47 percent. Medicare itself makes up about 20 percent of total health care spending (Levit et al. 1998). Most of the policy debate, especially in recent years, has concentrated on how to contain public sector medical spending. The focus on Medicare, in particular, has enabled policymakers to implicate demographic changes as the dominant threat to containing health care costs. But this emphasis on both the public sector and the elderly is extremely misleading.

In the first place, the cost of medical care paid by the federal government is overwhelmingly determined in private markets. For example, from 1970 to 1993, the cost of private medical insurance increased at an average annual rate of 13.4 percent, almost equal to that for Medicare, at 13.7 percent (Levit et al. 1996). It is therefore the failure to contain the costs of private health care spending that threatens not only Medicare's long-term viability but overall government spending as well: the long-term projections for the entire federal budget have been driven to explosive levels by these rising health care costs, which have their origin in the waste and inefficiency of private sector health care. For example, the Congressional Budget Office (CBO) regularly publishes long-term projections that show a rocketlike upsurge in the national debt a few decades from now; 1998's numbers have the debt reaching 100 percent of gross domestic product (GDP) in the mid-2040s.[1] These projections then become the basis for debates about how to cut entitlement spending or federal spending generally, what to do with near-term budget surpluses (pay down the debt), and related issues. But few seem to notice that health care inflation is the driving force behind these unsustainable projected spending increases. If this fact were more widely known, much of the debate about how to keep the budget deficit from ballooning in the next few decades would soon be replaced by a discussion of health care reform.

One way to sort out the effect of health care inflation from that of demographic changes is to make separate projections of future household income under different assumptions about these trends. For example, we can project household income under the assumption that health care spending rises only as a result of the aging of the population and per capita GDP growth. We can also project a scenario in which the age composition of the population remains the same. When we do this (see chapter 2), the effect of population aging, including the baby boomers' retirement, is significant but not very threatening: the reduction in the average family's after-tax income in 2030 attributable to demographic changes is about 6 percent, still leaving that family with an after-tax income that is more than 30 percent higher, in real terms, than it is today. Thus, the demographic changes alone still allow for a healthy growth of after-tax income even while increasing taxes to finance the retirement and health care of the baby boom generation.

The effect of rising health care costs, however, based on past rates of increase, is much greater. The average family would see its after-tax, after-

---

1. It is worth noting that the CBO's projections from March 1997, two years ago, showed the debt reaching 100 percent of GDP 20 years earlier, in the mid-2020s. This is an enormous change in the long-term forecast from one year to the next.

health-care income reduced by 14 percent, as compared to a scenario in which health care costs were brought under control. This would wipe out much of the income gain that would accrue to households from three decades of economic growth. Moreover, most of this reduction—about two-thirds—would come not from increasing taxes for Medicare or Medicaid but from increased costs of private sector medical care. Again, this illustrates that the problem so commonly attributed to entitlement spending is in fact a problem of cost control in the private health care sector.

But even the foregoing analysis overstates the effect of an aging population on health care spending, because it assumes that such spending increases directly with the proportion of elderly in the population. In other words, total health care spending is projected by applying the current cost of health care for elderly and nonelderly citizens to a population that contains a higher proportion of elderly. But this is an extrapolation from micro- to macro-data that does not necessarily reflect the real world. It may be that as a country's population ages, other measures are taken to reduce spending on the nonelderly population or to increase the productivity or efficiency of the health care system as a whole. This appears to be the case in other developed countries. In fact, the almost total lack of a relationship between the aging of the population and total health care spending is striking, not only for cross-sectional comparisons between countries in a given year but also in terms of the growth of health care spending in each country over time.[2]

Table 3-1 lists the percentage of GDP spent on health care for 18 countries in the Organization for Economic Cooperation and Development, including the United States (OECD 1997), and the percentage of the population over 65. There is no obvious relationship between the age of the population and health care spending. In Sweden, for example, 17.3 percent of the population is over 65—a proportion that the United States is not expected to reach for another 25 years. Yet it spends only 7.2 percent of its income on health care, or about half of what we spend. A number of other countries with older populations—namely, Austria, Italy, Norway, and Britain—also spend less than the average (8.1 percent for the group). Figure 3-1 shows this lack of relationship in a scatter plot (OECD 1997).

The growth of health care spending also appears to be unrelated to the

---

2. Among health policy analysts, this point has been emphasized most recently by Marmor and Oberlander 1998 and Rasell 1997.

Chapter Three

Table 3-1. Health Care Spending and the Aging of the Population

	1995		1960		*Increase in % of population over 65*	*Increase in health spending as % of GDP*
	% of population over 65	*Health spending as % of GDP*	*% of population over 65*	*Health spending as % of GDP*		
Australia	11.9	8.6	8.4	4.8	3.5	3.8
Austria	14.7	7.9	11.9	4.2	2.8	3.7
Canada	12	9.7	7.6	5	4.4	4.7
Finland	14.1	7.7	7.5	3.5	6.6	4.2
France	15.2	9.9	11.6	4.2	3.6	5.7
Germany	15.2	10.4	10.2	4.7	5	5.7
Greece	15.9	5.8	8.1	2.3	7.8	3.5
Iceland	11.5	8.2	8.2	3.5	3.3	4.7
Italy	16.1	7.7	9.2	3.5	6.9	4.2
Japan	14.2	7.2	5.7	2.9	8.5	4.3
Netherlands	13.2	8.8	9	3.9	4.2	4.9
New Zealand	11.4	7.1	8.7	4.4	2.7	2.7
Norway	15.9	8	11	2.8	4.9	5.2
Spain	15	7.6	8.1	1.5	6.9	6.1
Sweden	17.3	7.2	11.8	4.2	5.5	3
Switzerland	14.3	9.8	11.1	3.3	3.2	6.5
United Kingdom	15.8	6.9	11.7	3.8	4.1	3.1
United States	12.4	14.2	8.8	5	3.6	9.2

*Percent increase from 1960 to 1995.
Source: OECD 1997.

aging of the population over time, as shown in figure 3–2. This graph plots the increase, in percentage points, in the share of GDP devoted to health care spending as a function of the rate of growth of the elderly population. It is clear that countries that experience a faster growth in their proportion of senior citizens do not necessarily increase their health care spending, as a proportion of their income, any faster than other countries whose population is aging at a slower pace.[3]

These trends do not mean, however, that the aging of the population has no effect on per capita health care costs. Clearly there must be some effect: in

3. Getzen (1992) has shown both of these relationships for the years 1960–88. He also found that the age composition of the population was not significant in explaining the differences in health care spending across countries when per capita income was included in the regression. The same was true when the dependent variable was the rate of growth of health care expenditures, regressed against the growth of the elderly population.

Entitlements for the Elderly

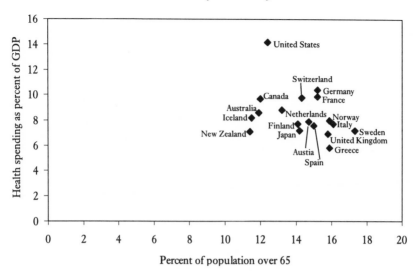

Figure 3-1. Health Care Spending and the Aging of the Population, 1995

the United States, for example, health care spending on the average senior citizen is about four times the average for the rest of the population (Waldo et al. 1989). But the rate at which the population ages is rather slow compared with all changes in other variables that have caused health care spending to grow fairly rapidly as a share of GDP in recent decades. To look at it from the other side, it is plausible that differences in cost control measures are important enough to swamp the effect of demographics.

Some have argued that the most expensive effects of aging are yet to come, as life expectancy increases and people spend a larger proportion of their lives in need of expensive medical intervention. Indeed, projections of the effect of longevity on Medicare spending typically assume that rates of disability and the need for health care remain the same for the various age groups as life spans increase (see, e.g., Lubitz, Beebe, and Baker 1995). That is, they assume that the medical needs of a typical 70-year-old will be the same 30 years from now, when people are living much longer, as they are today. But recent research has indicated that as people live longer lives, they may also live healthier lives, and the onset of disability is postponed and compressed into fewer years at the end of life (see, e.g., Vita et al. 1998; Manton, Corder, and Stallard 1997; and Fries 1989).

In the major debates over public policy, however, demography is still destiny, and "entitlements for the elderly" are the problem that threatens to drive

Chapter Three

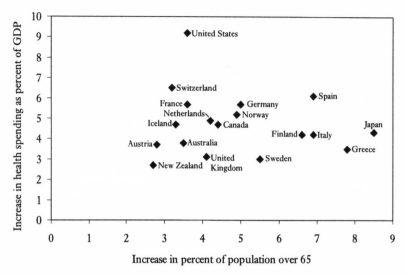

Figure 3-2. Percent Increase in Health Care Spending and the Aging of the Population, 1960-95

the nation to economic ruin. In this simplified world, we are told that there are only two measures that can save us: serious cuts in those entitlements or increasing the efficiency of the health care system through continuing privatization.

The Wrong Direction

The costs of caring for a larger elderly population in the next few decades would be manageable, and still allow for a sizable increase in everyone's living standards, if health care inflation could be brought under control. The majority of policymakers do not share this view, but they do recognize the need to tame health care inflation (Schieber, Poullier, and Greenwald 1993).

In the conventional view of many policymakers, the "moral hazard" inherent in our fee-for-service system has been responsible for exceedingly high health care inflation. In a fee-for-service system, doctors or other providers are paid a set fee for any particular service they perform, such as an operation or patient visit. This arrangement encourages unnecessary medical procedures, it is argued, from expensive diagnostic tests to operations. Combined with the guaranteed payment of private insurance (or public insurance, in the case of Medicare), we have what economists call a moral hazard: providers have an incentive to increase services, and patients have no particular reason to avoid unnecessary utilization.

There is some truth to this argument, but it does not seem to capture the most important elements of the picture. A number of other developed countries have fee-for-service systems—for example, Germany, France, Canada, Austria, and Switzerland. As can be seen in table 3-1, none have suffered either the high per capita costs or the rapid growth of health care spending that we have.

As will be seen, American health care suffers from more profound irrationalities than the moral hazard inherent in a fee-for-service or a third-party payment system. Unfortunately, we are currently in the midst of an experiment with managed care that is exacerbating some of these irrationalities and introducing new ones. Among the subjects of this experiment are the elderly, as the number of Medicare beneficiaries enrolled in health maintenance organizations (HMOs) continues to soar.

The Wrong Incentives

The rationale for managed care is that it can restructure incentives in a way that reduces the moral hazard of a traditional fee-for-service system and eliminate other inefficiencies. The objective is accomplished by some combination of insurance, management, and the provision of health services within the same organization. An HMO, for example, may contract with individual doctors, associations of doctors, or other providers, or it may hire physicians and health care professionals directly as employees. The HMO collects premiums from enrollees, and it makes a profit to the extent that the total of premiums exceeds its spending on health care services. Some managed-care organizations contract with providers on a per capita basis, a system called capitation. In this method, doctors or other providers may be paid a set fee per enrollee, regardless of the cost of medical services each person ends up incurring. This provides a strong incentive for the doctor or provider to minimize the amount of resources used per patient.

Managed care is not inherently bad or unworkable; its success or failure depends on the incentive structures built into the system, who is doing the managing, and for what purposes. Indeed, some kind of coordination between primary care physicians, specialists, and other providers—what some analysts have called "clinically managed care" (see Light 1994)—would be a necessary part of any rationally ordered health care system. At the other end of

Chapter Three

the spectrum is the profit-driven management that hires a highly paid administrator who cuts costs by replacing registered nurses with "patient care assistants." It is the latter kind of managed care that has been growing most rapidly, with results that can be dangerous as well as wasteful.

The biggest waste results from the very goal of private insurance, which is inevitably to insure the healthy and avoid the sick. The result for health care cost containment is starkly illustrated in the case of managed care in Medicare. Medicare pays the HMO or other managed-care organization a fee for each enrollee, which varies by region but is based on the cost of an average Medicare beneficiary. The average payment to HMOs is currently about $5,300 a year (HCFA 1997a). There is big money to be made here. Nineteen percent of all Medicare patients cost the program nothing in a typical year, and fully half of all patients cost less than $500 a year; this healthier half of Medicare patients is responsible for about 1 percent of all Medicare spending. On the other hand, the sickest 4 percent of Medicare patients—at more than $25,000 each—make up 46 percent of Medicare's costs (HCFA 1997b, 44). In this situation, the potential for "skimming"—enrolling the healthier patients and disenrolling, as much as possible, those who need expensive medical treatment—is enormous. It will dwarf all other ways of making a profit (with the possible exception of actual fraud, which also appears to have increased substantially in recent years).[4]

There is evidence that HMOs are actually pursuing such a strategy. A nationwide study found that Medicare HMOs enrolled significantly fewer patients who were very old or who suffered from heart disease, mental illness, or other health problems (Riley et al. 1996). A study of Florida Medicare HMO enrollees found that they were about one-third less costly than the average Medicare patient in the year before they joined the HMO. Those who disenrolled were found to be about 80 percent more expensive when they returned to fee-for-service Medicare than the average Medicare beneficiary (Morgan et al. 1997).[5] Senior citizens who receive Medicare coverage through HMOs also report a much higher incidence (13.3 percent vs. 4 percent in fee-for-service plans) of problems with access to care (Nelson et al. 1997), and

4. Federal investigations for health care fraud have risen more than fivefold in just five years, from 927 in 1992 to 4,688 in 1996 (Bellandi 1997). It is not known how much of this rise may be due to increased enforcement rather than a higher incidence of fraud.

5. A number of the studies cited here are summarized in Woolhandler and Himmelstein 1998.

they were found to receive fewer home care visits and had worse outcomes (Shaughnessey, Schlenker, and Hittle 1994). They were more likely to be discharged to nursing homes and less likely to be sent to rehabilitation units, since the HMO would generally have to cover rehabilitation costs but not long-term care (Retchin et al. 1997).

It appears that elderly patients who are sick have good reason to leave HMOs and return to fee-for-service Medicare, especially if they are poor. A recent study of medical outcomes comparing the two health care delivery systems found that the elderly in HMOs were about twice as likely to report a deterioration in their health over a four-year period than those receiving traditional fee-for-service care (Ware et al. 1996). This confirms earlier research, involving randomized control groups, that found that poor, high-risk patients in HMOs had a 21 percent higher risk of dying than those in a fee-for-service plan (Ware et al. 1986).

Medicare and Health Care Reform

The growth of managed care both inside and outside Medicare (as well as Medicaid) illustrates the dangers of relying on market forces, and especially private insurance, as an agent of health care reform. In fact, the very principles by which private insurance operates are in direct conflict with any attempt to provide universal health care for all citizens.

The goal of private insurers is not only to enroll those with the lowest risk, as in the case of Medicare HMOs, but to fragment the risk pool in a way that allows them to charge a premium that will exceed the expected health care costs of any particular risk group. Higher premiums will be charged for those who are older or have preexisting conditions or other health risks. If individuals had to purchase their own insurance throughout their lifetimes, they would typically face low premiums when they were young and healthy and find insurance unaffordable as they aged or developed health problems.

Even at the level of employer-based insurance, insurers use "experience rating" to determine the premiums for a particular employer, meaning that the premium is based on prior experience with health care costs at the company. This practice has led to serious problems at small firms, where the smaller number of workers means that premiums may vary considerably and be priced out of reach for a company whose employees have incurred higher-than-usual medical costs.

The private market thus does not really provide a mechanism by which people can insure against the costs associated with health problems in the distant or even intermediate future (see Cutler 1996). There is a growing fear among consumer advocates that this problem will worsen as insurers take advantage of more advanced methods for estimating risk—for example, DNA screening. One of the purposes of social insurance is to resolve these problems. It allows (and in most cases compels) people to pay when they are young and healthy for insurance that they are much more likely to use when they are older. At the same time, the pooling of risk across the entire population makes that insurance equally affordable to everyone without regard to risk status.

Medicare was created, in part, for these reasons, and the opening of Medicare to the operation of private insurance, through managed care, has introduced a different and antagonistic set of principles. As noted above, insurers have an enormous incentive to "cherry pick" the lower-risk patients. But even aside from that problem, there is a deliberate fragmentation of the risk pool in the proliferating variety of choices now offered to the elderly: competing HMOs, preferred-provider organizations, provider-sponsored organizations, and different fee-for-service options. The most extreme version of risk fragmentation is embodied in medical savings accounts, recently approved for Medicare. In this option the enrollee chooses a plan with a high deductible that insures against catastrophic illness. Since such a plan is generally cheaper than regular fee-for-service or managed-care insurance, the enrollee is allowed to accrue some of the difference in a medical savings account. The accounts accrue tax-free returns, and funds can be withdrawn to cover medical expenses. The plan seems guaranteed to draw the healthiest Medicare patients to private insurers, thus removing their contribution to Medicare's spending on the less-healthy elderly. Overall Medicare costs will increase, and the administrative burden of tracking the withdrawals and spending from the accounts will be formidable.

The options now available to senior citizens are so complex that those charged with administering the system have found that "even well-educated beneficiaries have difficulty understanding them all." With some 40 percent of senior citizens having "very limited ability to read and use printed materials" (Pear 1998), it is difficult to see how this neoclassical fascination with tailoring insurance policies to individual preferences is going to produce a net gain for anyone. More important, these measures illustrate the futility and indeed the destructiveness of trying to contain health care inflation by reducing demand at the level of the individual patient. The savings that are achieved are generally not worth the cost in terms of further reducing access to needed care or adding administrative waste to the system.

These are the two great problems of the American health care system: lack of access and waste. They are also its distinguishing irrationalities compared to other developed countries. The United States has 43 million people without health insurance, and yet we spend a larger share of our income than any country in the world on health care. At nearly 14.2 percent of GDP, our health care spending is in a league of its own: the average for the other OECD countries shown in table 3-1 is 8.1 percent. Since 1960, the share of U.S. GDP devoted to health care has grown by 9.2 percentage points; this compares to an average of 4.5 percentage points for the other developed countries (OECD 1997).

The United States also ranks 23rd out of 29 industrialized countries in infant mortality and is in the bottom third for life expectancy. The U.S. ranking has been falling steadily for decades, and it can be expected to decline further due to recent developments such as welfare reform, significant cost-shifting from employers to employees, declining employer-based coverage (EBRI 1997), and the increasing restrictiveness of managed care.

At the same time our health care system is saddled with enormous administrative costs. The number of administrative personnel in our health care system has grown by 2,000 percent since 1970, and the nonclinical share of health care spending seems to be rising with the shift to managed care. While the average HMO takes about 14 percent of premiums for overhead and profits, some of the largest and most successful take 20–26 percent (Corporate Research Group 1997). The superiority of social insurance in reducing administrative expenses is well known to economists and health policy analysts. A General Accounting Office study in 1991 estimated that we could save about 11 percent of total health care costs, or $110 billion today, by switching to a single-payer social insurance system like Canada's (GAO 1991). Other estimates have put the savings even higher (Woolhandler, Himmelstein, and Lewontin 1993). In Canada, administrative costs for the national health care system are about 0.9 percent, similar to our Social Security system, and for Medicare they are about 2 percent.[6]

---

6. This figure is not directly comparable to the administrative costs for HMOs, since the latter incur some medical administrative costs not resulting from insurance. However, adjusting for these differences would still leave Medicare with a small fraction of the administrative costs of the private sector.

Chapter Three

Among the developed countries discussed above that have been much more successful at containing health care inflation, all provide for universal care or something close to it. The experience of European health care systems shows that the most successful cost-saving measures have been supply-side interventions that are difficult to achieve outside a universal system (Saltman and Figueras 1998). The most important of these is global budgeting, which sets a limit on spending by hospitals or other subsectors of the system. Reducing excess hospital beds (the United States has about a third too many) and controlling the price of health supplies and the payment of professionals are also easier to accomplish within a universal system. The same is true for efficiency gains that can be achieved by substituting primary and outpatient care for inpatient care (Saltman and Figueras 1998).

Health economists and other analysts have often emphasized the role of new technologies in accelerating health care inflation (see Cutler 1996 and Weisbrod 1991). For many of these analysts, the problem is that these high-tech procedures are often deployed to the point where they have little or even zero marginal impact on medical outcomes. While this is undoubtedly true to some extent, there is still a question of what to do about it. Once a technology is available, it is difficult to contain its use, especially if that means refusing a potential cure to a patient in need. Here again, the more promising reforms would seem to be on the supply side: that is, the adoption of measures to reduce the development of costly technologies that are of limited value in reducing mortality or disability. In a profit- and market-driven health care system, the incentives to develop and apply such technologies are strong. Furthermore, without global budgets for capital expenditures, there is a tendency to overpurchase certain technologies. For example, the United States has about twice as many mammography machines as it needs (Brown, Kessler, and Reuter 1990).

There are demand-side interventions that offer enormous potential savings, although not the kind that are directed at reducing the demand among individuals through such disincentives as cost-sharing. The most promising strategies would seem be those that reduce medical need through public health and education; this approach would also have much more effect on helping people live longer, healthier lives. About 80 percent of our health care costs currently result from chronic conditions that occur between the age of 55 and the end of life (Fries et al. 1998), and there is strong evidence that chronic illness and disability during this period are correlated with living standards.

For example, those with favorable risk factors—which include higher income and education as well as exercise—have only one-fourth to one-half the amount of disability in the seventh and eighth decades of life (Fries et al. 1998). The considerable socioeconomic differences in risk factors associated with earlier onset of disability and chronic illnesses make a strong case for reducing inequalities of income and education as a matter of public health. No one has yet explored the health effects of current trends toward increasing income inequality continuing over the next few decades, but any such projection would certainly reinforce the argument that growing inequality, rather than population aging, poses the greater economic threat to future generations (House, Kessler, and Herzog 1990).

Even taking the distribution of income as given, there are numerous efforts that could enhance the quality of life while reducing health care costs. However, these would require a shift of resources to health promotion (Fries et al. 1998), and there is little incentive under our present system for investing in the necessary public education and outreach. In theory, HMOs and other managed-care organizations should have a stake in health promotion for their members. But their horizon is too short-term, and the turnover of doctors, as well as patients, is high. It seems that here, too, a universal system—especially one in which the government is the sole insurer—has much more potential, as well as the incentive structure, to accomplish these goals. The recent experience with tobacco legislation illustrates this point. Much of the impetus for this effort came from state governments seeking to recover the Medicaid costs that were incurred as a result of smoking-related illnesses. The curbs on tobacco companies' ability to promote new addictions, and other public health measures that may emerge from this confrontation, will have the potential to save millions of people from premature death and avoidable disability.

The establishment of universal social insurance for health care would also have important non-health-related economic benefits. The current attachment of health insurance to employment creates considerable inefficiencies in the labor market. The most obvious is "job-lock," where people remain in jobs that they would otherwise leave, simply for fear of losing their health insurance. The reduction in mobility for married men, for example, has been estimated at 26 percent (Madrian 1994). On the other side of the labor contract, the fixed cost of health insurance for employers predisposes them to increase hours rather than hire more employees (Cutler and Madrian

1996). Although this practice will not necessarily increase unemployment over the long run, it does contribute to widespread overwork and stress on the part of employees, many of whom report, for example, that they would like to have more time to spend with their families.

The current debate over entitlements for the elderly has managed to project an Orwellian inversion of reality. On the grounds of efficiency, equity, and cost containment, a universal, single-payer social insurance system is the clear winner. We know this not only as a matter of economic logic but from national and international experience as well. It is also clear from polling data that people want universal health care and would even be willing to pay higher taxes in order to achieve it.[7] In Medicare we have such a system for the elderly, although its coverage is incomplete.

A rational public discussion would focus on how to expand Medicare's coverage to meet the needs not only of the elderly but of the entire population. Instead, we have a debate about how to cut Medicare and a race to implement increasingly complex and administratively wasteful means of privatizing the insurance that it provides. Moreover, Medicare's problems in cost containment, which are wholly imported from the private sector, are used to project explosive growth not only for Medicare but for the entire federal budget. And finally, with a link no stronger than guilt by association, Social Security is dragged into the swamp of "unsustainable entitlement spending."

7. See, for example, a *New York Times*/CBS News poll conducted July 14–17, 1994. Some experts have taken the failure of President Clinton's attempt at health care reform in 1994 to mean that more sweeping measures, such as a single-payer social insurance system, are not politically feasible. But the long-run growth of health care costs cannot be sustained, so something will have to change. Given that there is still widespread public support for universal health care, it would seem that a social insurance system for health care is more feasible than the continuation of the status quo into the indefinite future.

4 | The Debate over the Consumer Price Index

IN DECEMBER 1996, the consumer price index (CPI) became the hottest topic in Washington. Government bureaucrats held standing-room-only press conferences in which they discussed esoteric methods of measurement and economic theory. The punditry offered its insights on the accuracy of the CPI on the Sunday morning talk shows. And the most closely guarded document in the nation's capital was the final report of the Boskin Commission, a body established by the Senate Finance Committee to evaluate the accuracy of the CPI.

What explains this sudden burst of interest in the fine points of constructing price indexes? At the time, both political parties were desperate to find ways to eliminate the federal budget deficit. The Republican Congress had set 2002 as a target for a balanced budget, and the Clinton administration had accepted it. But with the budget projections they had in hand, there didn't seem to be any politically viable path to reach their goal.

Enter the CPI. It is not clear who first recognized the importance of the CPI for the federal budget, but Federal Reserve Board Chairman Alan Greenspan deserves credit for bringing the issue to public prominence in the fall of 1994. Testifying before Congress, he called attention to long-standing problems with the CPI that could lead it to overstate the true rate of inflation by as much as 2.0 percentage points a year. He also pointed out that major areas of the federal budget, most importantly Social Security, are linked to the CPI because it is key to the size of cost-of-living adjustments (COLAs). Income tax brackets are linked to the CPI as well: income cutoffs for higher tax brackets move up each year by the rate of inflation shown by the CPI. Greenspan told Congress that if the CPI could be changed so that it recorded a lower rate of inflation, then the government would pay out less each year in benefits and would collect more in taxes. A reduction of just 1.0 percentage point would actually go most of the way toward balancing the budget.

This was just the news many members of Congress wanted to hear: they could balance the budget with a technical change in an obscure economic indicator. They would not have to raise anyone's taxes or cut a popular program like Social Security. All they had to do was tell the responsible agency, the Bureau of Labor Statistics (BLS), to get its act together.

There were some problems with this approach. The first was the logical one. A technical fix would not really make the deficit vanish: real people were going to lose real money. On the spending side, Social Security beneficiaries and other people who received indexed benefits would see reductions in their future benefits. On the tax side, people would pay higher taxes through the years as they were pushed into higher tax brackets as a result of a reduction in the CPI. In short, any reduction in the CPI's measure of inflation was going to cut Social Security and raise taxes.

The other problem was that it was not clear the CPI really did overstate inflation. The problems cited by Alan Greenspan and others had long been known to economists who studied price indexes. All of the issues raised in the recent debate over the CPI were mentioned in the report of the Stigler Price Commission, back in 1961. This commission, chaired by Nobel laureate George Stigler, was appointed by Congress to evaluate the accuracy of the nation's price statistics. Its report pointed to a series of problems that the BLS has been mostly able to address in the intervening 35 years. It was not clear that the remaining problems pushed the CPI in the same direction or led to an overstatement of the magnitude claimed by Greenspan.

To rally support for the idea of adjusting the CPI downward, the Senate Finance Committee created a commission consisting of five prominent economists, all of whom had previously testified that they believed the CPI substantially overstated inflation. It was chaired by Michael Boskin, the top economist in the Bush administration. In its final report, it concluded that the CPI overstates inflation by 1.1 percentage points a year. The estimate was not much of a surprise: it was the average of the estimates the commission members had given individually in their previous testimony before the Senate.

At the time the report was released, virtually all the knowledgeable people in Washington were sure that any budget agreement would include some downward adjustment in the CPI. The only question was how large the adjustment would be. But events unfolded differently. Congressional Democrats rallied against any downward adjustments, recognizing that a benefit cut had exactly the same impact regardless of how it was justified. Similarly, many Republicans objected to the plan, recognizing that it would lead to higher taxes. Finally, the budget picture changed substantially. Revenue collections ran well above projections, and spending was less than expected. The budget moved toward balance without any major cuts in government spending or increases in taxes, and the CPI was left in the hands of the BLS.

But in Washington no bad idea stays dead for long. At some point in the future, when the budget is strained again, enterprising members of Congress may dust off the Boskin report and revive the issue of construction of price indexes. Thus, it is important to deal with the issues raised by the commission.[1]

What Difference Does 1.1 Percent Make?

Before examining the Boskin Commission's case, it is worth briefly discussing the rationale for the indexation of Social Security and the effect a 1.1 percentage point cut in the size of the annual COLA would have for Social Security beneficiaries. Indexing Social Security and other benefits provides beneficiaries with protection against the impact of inflation. Retirees can thus plan for the future with a high degree of certainty that the purchasing power of their Social Security check will be nearly constant through their retirement. The alternative would be the system in place prior to 1973, which provided for a fixed nominal payment that could be adjusted insofar as the budget allowed and as political pressures dictated. Congress switched to indexation to provide retirees more certainty and because debates over benefit levels were consuming large amounts of time and dominating the political agenda. Many viewed the switch to indexation as a way to control benefits, since they had actually been rising considerably faster than the inflation rate over the prior 10 years. But even under the current indexation system, Congress *always* has the option to vote for less than full indexation any time budgetary considerations necessitate such a move.

At first glance, a 1.1 percentage point reduction in the COLA might seem relatively minor, but a more careful examination shows that the impact is quite large over time. Take the average couple in 1996, which received $13,407 in

---

1. At the time of this writing (May 1999), a group of senators, including Daniel Patrick Moynihan, was planning to introduce a Social Security proposal that called for reducing the annual COLA based on the conclusions of the Boskin Commission.

benefits. In the first year the impact of a 1.1 percentage point cut in the COLA would be a not-too-onerous reduction in benefits of $147. But in the fifth year the benefit reduction would exceed $720, for a cumulative cut of more than $2,300. The impact would continue to compound as the couple aged: in the 10th year it would exceed $1,300, and in the 20th year, $2,600, for a cumulative loss of more than $26,000.

In short, the Boskin-adjusted COLA amounts to a very significant reduction in benefits through time. And because the size of the benefit cut grows each year, the oldest beneficiaries will be the hardest hit. This group also tends to be the poorest, since people generally get poorer through their retirement years. So, even if Social Security cuts were necessary, the Boskin-adjusted COLA seems like a particularly bad way to bring about savings.

The Boskin Arithmetic

The Boskin Commission, in reaching its conclusion that the CPI overstated the true rate of inflation by 1.1 percentage points annually, cited four distinct sources of bias:

1. Substitution bias. The index, because it follows a fixed basket of goods and services, misses the savings that consumers can achieve by making substitutions for goods that are rising relatively rapidly in price. The commission estimated that this bias led the CPI to overstate inflation by 0.4 percentage points a year.

2. Retail outlet substitution bias. The CPI does not pick up the gains that consumers might get from shopping at discount stores or new outlets that offer better service. The commission put the size of this bias at 0.1 percentage points.

3. Quality bias. The commission argued that the CPI failed to accurately measure all the quality improvements in goods and services through time. Therefore, the CPI was treating higher prices attributable to quality improvements as inflation. The commission combined its estimate for this overstatement with the following category.

4. New goods bias. Many new goods experience rapid price declines soon after they first appear, but the CPI does not track new goods as soon as they emerge on the market. By missing these large price declines the CPI could overstate the true rate of inflation. In its final report, the commission estimated the combined impact of quality and new goods bias as 0.6 percentage points.

Some evidence exists for the commission's assessment in each case, but the fact that there are reasons for believing that the CPI might overstate inflation does not establish that it actually does, or by how much. There are also reasons for believing that the CPI may understate inflation, particularly for certain demographic groups such as the elderly. A comprehensive assessment of the CPI as a measure of consumer inflation must examine all aspects of the index, not just the ones that make it appear to err on one side.

Few economic indicators are used so pervasively as the CPI, and it is important to remember that it does not exist in isolation from other economic phenomena. If the CPI has a significant bias in either direction, then the consequences extend over a wide range of economic data, and economists will have to adjust large amounts of information and reexamine many accepted economic theories. We will also have to rewrite much of economic history. In other words, economists cannot have a CPI that is overstated for calculating COLAs but accurate everywhere else.

The Evidence for an Overstated CPI

Substitution Bias

The Boskin Commission is correct in its assessment that the CPI will tend to overstate inflation somewhat because it is a fixed-weight index that follows a fixed basket of goods and services. But its estimate of the size of the overstatement—0.4 percentage points—is slightly higher than can be supported by the existing evidence.

Substitution bias occurs when people increase their purchases of goods and services that are rising less rapidly in price and reduce purchases of items that are rising more rapidly. Since the CPI does not take these sorts of substitutions into account, it can tend to overstate the true rate of inflation.

The Boskin Commission broke down the substitution bias into two different types: "upper-level substitution bias," which results from failing to pick up a shift between broad categories of goods, such as from beef to chicken, and "lower-level substitution bias," which results from failing to pick up shifts within categories of goods, such as between types of chicken or types of beef.

The BLS has done a lot of work in the area of substitution bias, and it is able to give fairly precise estimates of the size of the bias that can result from using a fixed-weight index. In the case of upper-level substitution bias, the BLS has data on how consumption patterns actually shifted over the course

Chapter Four

of the year,[2] making it possible to calculate the extent to which the inflation rate would be affected if the CPI had actually picked up these substitutions.[3] This research indicates that the size of the upper-level substitution bias averaged 0.14 percentage points a year for the years 1988–95 (Aizcorbe and Jackman 1993, 1997). The number was pushed up somewhat by the big oil price increases associated with the Persian Gulf War in 1990; in a typical year of moderate, even inflation, which we have experienced in the late 1990s, the size of bias is just 0.11 percent.

The lower-level substitution bias is a bit more difficult to judge, since we don't have data on how consumption patterns have actually shifted. BLS research indicates that, if one assumes that a great deal of substitution takes place, then the size of this bias would be 0.25 percentage points a year. However, some of the substitutions implied by this estimate are implausible. For example, the estimate implies that people would switch from buying clothes washers to clothes dryers if the price of washers rose more rapidly than the price of dryers, or that they would switch from heart medicine to headache medicine if the latter rose less rapidly in price. A reasonable guess is that half of the substitutions implied by this estimate may be plausible, and therefore the size of lower-level substitution is probably about 0.13 percentage points annually. In early 1999, the BLS began calculating the CPI under the assumption that consumers make substitutions in response to changes in relative prices, such as switching between types of oranges. The agency's change should eliminate the lower-level substitution bias in the index.

Retail Outlet Substitution Bias

Retail outlet substitution bias has at most a small effect on the measured rate of inflation because it applies only to certain types of goods and only to the portion of sales that switched between retail outlets in a given year. The goods that are thought to be subject to this bias are items that are sold in traditional retail stores but can be sold in discount stores like Wal-Mart (appliances, clothes, household products, food, etc.); these goods make up ap-

2. These data are not usually available until November of the following year, which is why they cannot be integrated into a CPI that has to be produced on a monthly basis.

3. The accepted procedure among economists for incorporating the effect of substitutions is to use an average of the rate of inflation in the bundle of goods and services consumed at the beginning of the year and the rate of inflation in the bundle of goods and services purchased at the end of the year.

proximately 30 percent of the index. The CPI already measures prices in both places, but it misses the portion of sales in any given year that switches from traditional stores to discounters. Assuming the portion of switchers a year is 1.0 percent (it's not likely to be higher, for if it were, soon all goods would be purchased at discount stores), then the retail outlet bias would apply to 0.3 percent of the whole CPI (1.0 percent of 30.0 percent).

The next question is, how much of a gain does the typical consumer get from shopping at a discount store? It's not only a question of price: many customers view the gains from lower prices as being partially offset by lower service quality. In standard economic theory, these differences would be viewed as completely offsetting, since both stores continue to operate in the same market. But in reality, many traditional retail stores have been losing business or shutting down, so it is reasonable to believe that consumers see some gain, even after adjusting for differences in service, in discount stores. Assuming a 10.0 percent service-adjusted gain, the retail outlet substitution bias would be 0.03 percentage points annually, not a great deal to get worried about.

Even this amount is probably an overstatement, since it ignores effects that go the other way. Here are two examples. In many cases retail stores go out of business because their owners retire. In these cases consumers may prefer to shop at a store in their neighborhood but lose the opportunity when the store closes. This is a loss that would not be picked up in the CPI. The other example is probably somewhat more important. In many cases traditional retail stores have begun to lower their prices to become more price competitive with discounters, and they have often had to cut back on the quality of service to make the price cuts affordable.[4] The CPI would pick up the decline in prices but not the deterioration in service quality. It is possible, if not likely, that this source of understatement of inflation is as large as any overstatement that can be identified with retail outlet substitution bias.

Quality and New Goods Bias

Most of the Boskin Commission's estimate of CPI bias stems from the index's treatment of quality change and the failure to pick up price declines in new goods. A prominent example of this problem during the public debate on the CPI was the cellular phone. Due to an oversight, the BLS had failed to

---

4. A survey of retailers showed that they had reduced their sales staff by 10–30 percent in the 1990s (Steinhauer 1997).

Chapter Four

include the cellular phone in the CPI's basket of goods. Since cellular phones had become fairly common by 1996, and their price had dropped dramatically, this omission appeared to be a major blunder that exemplified BLS ineptitude. Closer examination revealed that the exclusion of cellular phones, while admittedly a serious mistake, would not have made much difference in the measure of inflation.[5] In fact, when we examine the basis of most of the Boskin Commission's estimates of quality and new goods bias more closely, it turns out that, like the cellular phone example, there really is not much there.

In everyday discussions it is common to make an argument based on an anecdote. Such arguments usually go nowhere, since it is often possible to present other anecdotes that have opposite implications. Economists generally try to avoid anecdotes in favor of evidence, yet in presenting its case for the size of the quality and new goods bias in the CPI, the Boskin Commission relies a great deal on anecdotes. Of the 0.61 percentage points of quality and new goods bias it attributed to the CPI, 0.17 percentage points rely primarily or exclusively on the commission's speculation based on anecdotal evidence.

For example, the commission concluded that food and beverages improved at an annual rate 0.3 percentage points more rapid than was picked up by the CPI. It arrived at this conclusion by noting:

> How much would a consumer pay to have the privilege of choosing from the variety of items available in today's supermarket instead of being constrained to the much more limited variety available 30 years ago? A conservative estimate of the extra variety and convenience might be 10 percent for food consumed at home other than produce, 20 percent for produce where the increased variety in winter (as well as summer farmers' markets) has been so notable, and 5 percent for alcoholic beverages where imported beer, microbreweries, and greatly improved distribution of imported wines from all over the world have improved the standard of living. (Senate Finance Committee 1996, 41–42)

In addition to relying excessively on anecdotes, the commission also sometimes misread evidence. For example, a study of the CPI's measurement of quality improvements in home appliances by commission member Robert Gordon found that the CPI showed a *lower* measured rate of inflation in these

---

5. Moulton and Moses (1997) examined the possible impact of the cellular phone on the overall CPI. They estimated that its inclusion in the market basket over the prior 10 years would have lowered the measured rate of inflation by at most 0.02 percentage points annually.

goods than an index he had constructed based on Sears catalogs. Nonetheless, the commission cited the Gordon study as evidence supporting an overstatement of inflation in the CPI's treatment of appliances. In another instance, the commission identified a bias associated with a service—automatic teller machines—that is mostly not even counted in the CPI.[6] In the case of nonprescription drugs and medical supplies, the commission provided no evidence whatsoever of an inflation overstatement. In short, the commission's report contained considerably less substance than one might have expected.

Sources of Understated Inflation in the CPI

While the Boskin Commission seemed determined to find every possible way in which the CPI might overstate the true rate of inflation, it did not put much effort into finding ways in which it might understate inflation. It turns out that the sources of understatement can also fill a long list.

For starters, it is not clear that the quality bias in the CPI always leads to an understatement of quality improvements and therefore an overstatement of inflation. The BLS already imputes a substantial amount of quality improvements in the goods and services it examines; in 1996 quality imputations lowered the rate of inflation measured by the CPI by 1.76 percentage points, from 4.7 percent to 2.9 percent.

The issue of quality in the CPI is not whether goods and services are getting better but rather how quickly. In the case of several goods and services, there is reason to believe that the CPI overstates the rate at which items are improving. A good example is automobiles, for which the CPI has included substantial adjustments for quality improvements since the mid-1960s. To determine the amount of quality improvement in new cars, the BLS asks the automobile manufacturers how much of their price increases each year are due to improved quality. The BLS then deducts this value from the actual increase in car prices to measure the amount of the increase due strictly to inflation. Since car manufacturers want to appear to be holding the line on prices, they have strong incentive to exaggerate the cost of quality improve-

---

6. Most of the services provided by automatic teller machines would not be included in the CPI because they are usually provided free of charge by banks to checking account customers that maintain a minimum balance. These services do bear a cost, and they are counted as a payment in lieu of interest in the gross domestic product (GDP) accounts. However, these services are not part of households' cash income and therefore are not among the goods and services that properly fall in the CPI's purview.

Chapter Four

ments. While the BLS does indeed make an effort to independently evaluate the cost of quality improvements, its ability to do so is limited by its access to information. This procedure thus seems more likely to produce an overstatement of quality improvements and an understatement of inflation.

A second product for which current procedures seem likely to produce an overstatement of quality improvement is computers. In February 1998, the BLS adopted a procedure for measuring computer prices that is already in place at the Commerce Department. The Commerce Department's price measure, using this procedure, shows that computer prices have been falling 40.0 percent per year. While computer prices are clearly falling rapidly, this is a remarkable rate of price decline. It implies that in five years, the equivalent of today's $2,500 computer will be selling for $194. Furthermore, such a rapid rate of price decline does not seem consistent with the pattern of growth in computer sales. Sales have been increasing at the rate of about 16 percent a year,[7] and thus demand would have to be very unresponsive to price declines, or inelastic, if the true price of computers has actually been falling 40 percent a year. Even Boskin Commission member Robert Gordon has suggested that 15–20 percent is a more plausible rate of price decline for computers.[8]

A third case in which BLS procedures seem likely to understate inflation is in the treatment of generic drugs. Since January 1995, the BLS has used a procedure in which generic drugs are treated as identical to the name-brand drugs with which they compete, meaning that there is often a large price decline associated with generic drugs entering the market. While generic drugs provide large savings, many physicians believe that, because the quality control for the generic drug may not be as careful as for the branded drugs, and because inert substances may differ between branded drugs and generic drugs,[9] the generic drugs are not as good for some of their patients. For these reasons, treating the generic drug as identical to the branded drug will overstate the true price decline associated with the entrance of a generic drug into the market. The procedure recommended in an article on this issue by Boskin

7. These figures are based on unpublished data from the Information Technology Industry Council in Washington, D.C.

8. "Some Experts Say Inflation Is Understated," *New York Times*, November 6, 1997, p. D1.

9. Generic drugs are determined by the Food and Drug Administration to be identical to the branded drug in their active component. This active component is generally mixed with other substances to make the pill that is marketed.

The Debate over the Consumer Price Index

Commission member Zvi Griliches is to assume that half the price difference between the branded drug and the generic drug is attributable to a genuine price difference and that the other half is due to a real quality difference (Griliches and Cockburn 1994).

Apart from these narrow methodological issues, a broader set of quality issues might lead to an understatement of the rise in the cost of living. Many of these might be hard to quantify, but they can nonetheless be important in terms of how people value goods and services.

For example, airplanes are in general much fuller today than in the period prior to deregulation, and so passengers generally sit in full rows without empty middle seats. While the CPI would pick up the price declines associated with deregulation, it would not pick up any reduction in service quality associated with more-crowded flights.[10]

Another source of possible understatement of inflation is the failure to pick up the search costs incurred by consumers in finding the lowest price. A good example is telephone service. Prior to the breakup of AT&T's monopoly, consumers spent little time choosing their phone service, since they didn't have much choice. Today, consumers are bombarded with advertisements, mailings, and phone solicitations for various long-distance services, and while the price reduction is picked up in the CPI, the value of the time consumers spend evaluating plans is not. Similar search costs would be involved with any service that had previously been provided by a monopoly, such as garbage collection or even electricity.

A different sort of example arises with television. The Boskin Commission identified cable television as a source of large gains to consumers that is not fully picked up in the CPI. While this may be true for some people, it also is a source of loss for many consumers. In many cities, entertainment formerly available on free television, such as a lot of sports programming, can now be seen only on cable. As a result, viewers who attached great value to these once-free broadcasts must now pay a monthly cable fee in order to watch the same entertainment. The CPI does not pick up this additional expense.

In fact, there are whole categories of new needs created by technology that the CPI will not pick up. For example, the telephone is now a virtual

---

10. The CPI actually missed much of the price decline associated with discount fares, but a new methodology put in place in 1992 should more effectively measure these price reductions.

Chapter Four

necessity, and a household without one today is much worse off than was a household without one in 1920. Similarly, now that cars have become the dominant form of transportation, our cities and suburbs have been designed to accommodate car ownership, and people without cars are far worse off now than they would have been 60 years ago. A current example is the Internet. While it offers enormous new opportunities, it will also impose new costs (buying a computer with Internet access, paying connect fees). As the Internet becomes a more common means of communication, those without access will be increasingly cut off from the people they need to contact.

These are just a few examples in which the development of technology and changes in society have created new needs for households. There is no simple way in which these additional costs can be included in the CPI, but the CPI is understating the increase in the cost of living if it excludes them altogether, as is currently the case. The Boskin Commission chose not to examine this set of issues, but if the intention is to make the CPI a genuine cost-of-living index, then there is no justification for ignoring them.

Inflation for Whom?

The Boskin Commission also gave short shrift to the question of whether inflation rates differ among demographic groups. While there is some evidence that they do (e.g., Jorgenson and Slesnick 1983), this is an area that needs more research.

The commission seems inadvertently to have made the case that there are large differences in inflation rates across demographic groups. By emphasizing new goods that experience rapid price declines, such as cellular phones, the Internet, and airplane phones, it identified falling prices that disproportionately benefit high-income people. For the most part, middle- and lower-income consumers cannot afford to purchase these goods until after they have already fallen substantially in price, and at that point they are likely to be incorporated in the CPI. Thus, the failure to include new items immediately in the CPI may lead to little inaccuracy in measuring the rate of inflation experienced by most consumers, since they are not purchasing items like cellular phones when they first appear on the market.[11] However, not including

---

11. According to the standard economic theory on which the CPI is based, the value of a good to a consumer is the highest price that he or she would be willing to pay for it. Therefore, if middle-income consumers are unwilling to buy cellular phones until their

these items may lead to a substantial overstatement of the rate of inflation experienced by high-income consumers. The policy implication of this point is that, if the actual rate of inflation for the wealthy is lower, the cutoffs for the top tax brackets, which are raised each year in line with the CPI, may be rising too high. For example, the income cutoff for a single individual to be taxed at a 39.6 percent rate instead of 36.0 percent should perhaps be $250,000 instead of $275,000. Thus, high-income people may be paying less in taxes than would be the case if the tax brackets had been indexed to a CPI that accurately measured their rate of inflation.

The other group that probably experiences a different rate of inflation than the overall population is the elderly. They tend not to be big Internet users, nor are they likely to take advantage of many of the new products with rapidly falling prices cited by the Boskin Commission. They are big consumers of health care, though, which until recently experienced a much more rapid rate of inflation than the overall CPI.

A separate elderly index that the BLS has been tabulating for a number of years shows that the rate of inflation experienced by the elderly over the period from 1984 to 1996 was 0.3 percentage points higher on average than the overall CPI.[12] The Boskin Commission noted the existence of this index but dismissed its findings as inconclusive (Senate Finance Committee 1996, 71). The commission is correct that the BLS index is not a comprehensive CPI for the elderly; to make it so would require analyzing exactly what goods and services the elderly consume and where they purchase them—in essence

---

price falls below $100, then $100 is exactly the value they place on a cellular phone. Therefore, the fall in the price of a cellular phone from $1,000 to $100 provides them with no gain whatsoever, since they are unwilling to purchase the phone at prices in this range. It is only after the price falls below $100, and they would have purchased the phone in any case, that they will experience any gains from further price declines. On the other hand, a wealthy person, who would have been willing to pay $1,000 for a cellular phone, will experience gains throughout this whole range.

12. Social Security benefits are actually indexed to the CPI-W, an index that is designed to measure the rate of inflation experienced by wage and clerical workers. This index has risen on average 0.1 percentage points a year less rapidly than the CPI-U, which is designed to measure the inflation rate experienced by all urban consumers. The CPI-U is the measure most often referred to in the media. The gap between the two indexes, plus the gap between the CPI-U and the experimental elderly index, implies that the index constructed to measure the rate of inflation experienced by the elderly has actually risen 0.4 percentage points a year more rapidly than Social Security benefits.

creating a second CPI. The BLS index is at best suggestive of possible differences between the rate of inflation for the elderly and for the rest of the population. However, if Congress were genuinely concerned that Social Security COLAs did not correspond to the true rate of inflation experienced by the elderly, instructing the BLS to conduct a full CPI for the elderly seems the best way to answer the question—or at least better than appointing a commission of five economists to examine the issue in their spare time.

A final point is worth noting about the cost of living for the elderly: the treatment of Medicare premiums in the CPI. Medicare provides for the majority of health care expenditures for people over 65, although beneficiaries still have to pay premiums to cover part of the costs of the program. At present, these premiums are about $45 per month, or slightly more than $500 per year, a significant sum for many of the elderly. A typical women over 65 living alone has an annual income of less than $10,000. Several plans in the recent budget debate would have raised this premium significantly, in some cases more than doubling it. While this would have been a substantial bite out of the income of most senior citizens, the CPI would not have picked up the higher premium, because Medicare is viewed as a government subsidy. The increase in the premium is treated as a reduction in the size of the subsidy, and such reductions are not treated as an increase in the cost of living.

Had the proposals to balance the budget through a downward adjustment to the CPI gone into place, Social Security beneficiaries would have seen a reduction in their COLA precisely at a time when their actual cost of living was rising far more rapidly than that of the general population. This would have been cruel treatment indeed of the nation's elderly.

The Implications of an Overstated CPI

In order to find a backdoor route to a balanced budget, many politicians were eager to embrace the claim that the CPI was overstated. However, many economists endorsed the idea as well. What they failed to notice, for the most part, was that changing the measure of inflation had implications far beyond its impact on the budget.

The CPI factors into almost all of the nation's economic data, and so, if it is substantially overstated, then most of the other data will have to be adjusted to remove the effects of this overstatement. Most immediately, if the CPI is overstated by 1.1 percentage points a year, then economic growth has been understated by virtually the same amount, due to the fact that most of the price data used to distinguish between inflation and real economic growth in measures of GDP actually come from the BLS calculations for the CPI. If the BLS has been overstating inflation in the CPI, then the Commerce Department has been overstating the amount of inflation in its measure of GDP growth. And if the Boskin Commission's conclusion is correct, then GDP growth has actually been about 1.1 percentage points a year more rapid than current data indicate.[13] Furthermore, the CPI overstatement also means that productivity growth has been understated by the same amount.

These changes in turn affect many other areas of economic research. For example, we will have to reexamine all macroeconomic work relating savings or other factors to economic growth, as well as some of the profession's core theories about lifetime saving and consumption behavior. If the Boskin Commission is correct, individuals must consume far less early in their lives and far more later in their lives than current data indicate, since we have been understating the increase in real income and consumption through time when we make comparisons with the CPI.

We will also have to recalculate studies of the gains from deregulation. It is standard in these studies to compare price trends in the deregulated industries with the overall CPI (e.g., Crandall and Ellig 1996). If the true rate of inflation is actually 1.1 percentage points a year less than is indicated by the CPI, then the gains from deregulation have been vastly overstated in these studies. For example, if airline prices have risen by 30 percentage points less

13. The real growth rate is calculated by breaking the growth in nominal GDP into a portion due to inflation and a portion due to an actual increase in the production of goods and services. If the nominal growth in GDP is 5.0 percent, and inflation is calculated at 3.1 percent, then the real growth rate is the difference, or 1.9 percent. But if the inflation rate was overstated and the true inflation rate is actually 1.1 percent less, or 2.0 percent, then the real growth rate would be 3.0 percent.

The Commerce Department calculates some consumption components by itself, so not all the bias in the CPI would appear in the consumption portion of GDP. Also, the GDP index is not a fixed-weight index, so it would not be subject to the upper-level substitution bias in the CPI. In addition, the GDP numbers also include measures of investment, government expenditures, and net exports. However, Gordon (1990a) presents evidence that the bias in the measurement of investment expenditures is every bit as large as for consumption. Most categories of government expenditures are not even subject to price measurement, and net exports comprise goods with prices measured elsewhere under consumption or investment. Therefore, it is a reasonable first approximation that any overstatement in the CPI translates almost completely into an understatement of economic growth.

than the overall CPI in the 20 years since deregulation, then economists would attribute this 30 percent price decline to deregulation in the industry. However, if an accurate CPI would have shown 1.1 percentage points less inflation each year, then airline prices have declined by only about 5.5 percent against an accurately measured CPI. (A 1.1. percentage point annual overstatement compounds to a 24.5 percent cumulative overstatement over 20 years.)

Few, if any, of the economists who embraced the Boskin Commission's conclusions were prepared to carry through its implications for economic research. In fact, even the members of the commission did not apply its conclusion about the CPI to their own work. In 37 published works in which an overstatement in the CPI would have affected research problems, in only 6 articles was the issue noted and in only 1 was an adjustment made (Baker 1997, 151). Apparently some economists were content to view the CPI as overstated for budgetary purposes but accurate when it affected important research findings. This was perhaps one reason why the political impact of these economists' views was limited.

Perhaps the greatest irony of the Boskin Commission quest was that the logical implication of their conclusion was exactly the opposite of the policy that it was supposed to support. If the CPI were overstated by 1.1 percentage points, then real incomes must have been rising 1.1 percentage points more rapidly than current data indicate. This conclusion is inescapable, because real income growth is defined as the growth in nominal income minus the inflation rate. If the true inflation rate is 1.1 percentage points less than the CPI indicates, then real income *must* be growing 1.1 percentage points more. If this is the case, it has to have been true for some time, since the CPI is probably no more inaccurate now than it has ever been. (By virtually all accounts the BLS has improved its methods considerably over the last 40 years.)

The implication of this point is that, if income has been growing more rapidly over the last 40 years than we thought, then we must have been much poorer 40 years ago.[14] Adjusting past income numbers in accordance with the

---

14. To illustrate this point, suppose that your income today is $40,000. If your income has doubled over the last 10 years, then you know that your income 10 years ago was $20,000. But if it turns out that your income actually grew more rapidly—that it tripled over the last 10 years—then 10 years ago it would have been just $13,333. The more rapid the growth, the lower the starting point.

The Debate over the Consumer Price Index

Boskin Commission's conclusion leads to the discovery that most families in the United States were living below the current poverty line as recently as 1960. Going back further to 1953, the typical family had to have been living at an income level that was about 80 percent of the government's official poverty line (see figure 4-1).

If we adjust our growth numbers going backward, we also have to adjust them going forward by the same amount, meaning that real wages and income will grow far more rapidly in the future than current data indicate. Adjusting the wage projections in the Social Security trustees' report in this way leads to the conclusion that the average annual wage in the year 2030 will be over $56,000 in 1998 dollars, compared with about $25,000 in 1996 (see figure 4-2). Thus, under this scenario our children will be far better off than we could have possibly hoped had the CPI been accurate. Under normal circumstances, it is almost impossible to imagine a set of economic policies that could increase real income growth at.the rate of 1.1 percentage points a year; securing gains even one-tenth this large would be viewed as an enormous success.

This is the incredible irony of the Boskin Commission's conclusion. If it is right, then most of the people currently receiving Social Security spent most of their lives in poverty. In turn, our children and grandchildren will be far richer than we could have ever hoped. Under this view of the past and

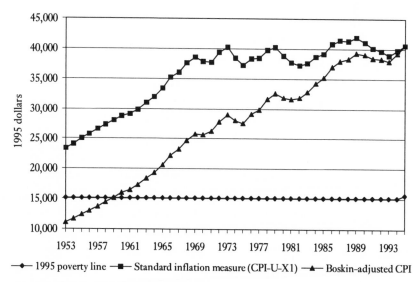

Figure 4-1. Real Median Family Income, 1953–94, Under Two Views of the Consumer Price Index

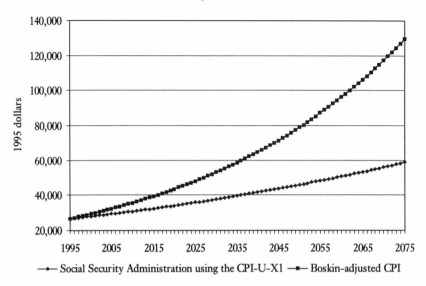

Figure 4-2. Projected Real Wages, 1995-2075, Under Two Views of the Consumer Price Index

future, it seems absurd for us to cut benefits for the elderly in order to make our children and grandchildren even richer. Such upward redistribution does not make much sense morally, nor would this sort of argument be likely to get far politically.

The Boskin Commission's Failed Case

The U.S. Senate established the Boskin Commission to provide cover for a political agenda. Cutting Social Security and other indexed benefits, along with a gradual increase in income taxes, was one way to get to a balanced budget. The proponents of this path could have chosen to argue their case before Congress and the nation. Instead they found a group of economists who they hoped would provide them with a way of hiding their real agenda behind a purely technical interest in correcting errors in government data.

For a variety of reasons, their political agenda did not carry the day, and the Boskin Commission's conclusions failed to carry the day among economists. Those who closely examined its claims found the evidence to be weak or nonexistent. The BLS has worked hard over the years to detect problems with the CPI and to make the necessary improvements. The commission's report did not provide reason to believe that it had done a better job than that agency.

Furthermore, virtually no one in the economics profession was willing to accept the radical reassessment of economic theory and history that the commission's conclusion required.

Finally, the commission's conclusion had such radical implications for the issue of generational equity that it undermined the policy the commission was intended to further. Discovering that our parents and grandparents lived in poverty and that our children and grandchildren will be relatively wealthy had a tendency to undermine the idea of cutting benefits for the former in order to rescue the latter. If, as the Boskin findings imply, our children and grandchildren will be rich, there is little point in worrying about them. As was said during the debate over the commission's report, "If Boskin is right, the future is bright."

5 | The Glories of Privatization

ACCORDING TO THE PROPONENTS of privatizing Social Security, if a minimum wage worker were allowed to put just 5 percentage points of his Social Security payments into a retirement account instead, he could retire a millionaire. Furthermore, we could rid ourselves of the huge burden Social Security will impose on our children and grandchildren. Only people who loved government bureaucracy could oppose these outcomes.

The proponents of privatization make a pretty attractive pitch for their policy. Their basic story is that a lot of people have made a lot of money in the stock market in recent years. If we just got rid of this antiquated government program, Social Security, those who have been left out could share in the riches as well.

But the problems with privatization set in as soon as you start asking about the details. For example, there is the small problem of financing the transition to a privatized system. If people stopped paying 5.0 percentage points of their Social Security tax to the government and put it in private accounts instead, how is the government going to make up the lost revenue? Currently, 5.0 percentage points of the payroll tax is about $180 billion a year. Without this revenue, the government would have to either raise taxes, cut other spending, or run a deficit. Most proponents of privatization have not been eager to discuss which of these routes they advocate.

The privatizers also have not been eager to make their projected stock returns consistent with the projected economic growth rates in the report of the Social Security trustees. The only reason that the Social Security fund has a long-term deficit is that the projected rate of economic growth over the next 75 years is less than half the rate of the last 75. But in spite of that bearish forecast, the privacy advocates expect Wall Street to do every bit as well over the next 75 years as it did before.

There are other problems with the privatizers' plans that can get lost in the details. For example, how will the system be run? Enormous efficiencies are associated with having a single, centralized system like Social Security. If the privatizers have their way, we will get dozens, hundreds, possibly thousands of separate funds in which people can park their savings. Will employers be required to make arrangements with whatever funds their workers happen to choose, or will workers have to accept whatever fund, or funds, their employers select? In the latter case, will workers have to switch funds when they switch jobs?

Also, how will the government decide which funds qualify for the privatized system? It is important to remember that the proposal being pushed is not really "privatization" but rather a system of government-mandated saving. Under this system the government will be forcing people, often against their will, to place their money in some type of approved account, and the privatizers have not explained exactly how the government will determine which funds will qualify. They also differ on how the government will regulate the system, or if the government will provide guarantees in the event that a particular fund does badly or is subject to fraud or embezzlement.

The privatizers also are not always clear on how they will ensure that the money will actually be there for people when they retire. At present, it is not possible to borrow against future Social Security benefits; how will the privatizers prevent people from borrowing against their own savings? And if they can borrow, then what will be left for retirement? Also, what will happen when people hit retirement age? Can they just spend all their money at once on a new boat or a big trip? If so, then why did the government force them to save all those years? If not, then how will the government regulate these accounts through retirement?

The answers to these questions are not simple, but two things are plain: privatizing will have to involve the creation of a massive regulatory structure that would oversee large portions of the nation's financial system, and the government will end up monitoring the personal savings and spending behavior of virtually every worker and retiree in the nation.

But the advocates of privatization would rather not dwell on the details. After all, there are riches to be made in the stock market. Let's just privatize Social Security and let the good times roll.

Chapter Five

A Happy Market, an Unhappy Economy

The most important flaw in the case for privatization is its assumption about the performance of the stock market. The assumed rate of return is key, because it is easy to present a story in which everyone gets rich if the annual rate of return is high enough. What is a reasonable rate of return to assume for the stock market over the next 75 years, the planning horizon for Social Security?

The privatizers generally assume that the stock market will grow about as rapidly in the future as it has in the past (see Carter and Shipman 1996; Kotlikoff and Sachs 1997; Feldstein and Samwick 1997).[1] In most cases it is reasonable to assume that the future will be like the past, but this is not one of them. The report of the Social Security trustees assumes that the economy will grow by less than 1.5 percent a year on average over the next 75 years, considerably lower than the 3.0 percent average rate of the previous 75 years. If the economy managed to grow at the same rate over the next 75 years as it did over the last 75, the Social Security fund would be virtually in balance, and no one would be worrying about it. It seems reasonable to expect of the privatizers that they accept the same assumptions about economic growth when making projections of stock returns as they do when they discuss the prospects of Social Security. To do so changes the picture enormously.

1. Kotlikoff and Sachs (1997) and Feldstein and Samwick (1997) actually skip any direct discussion of the stock market at all. They discuss the expected returns from privately invested funds as though workers were directly buying physical capital and receiving the average rate of return in that category. This implies that workers are directly purchasing factories or machinery with their retirement savings accounts. There is no mechanism in the economy in which workers can directly purchase physical capital in this way, nor do these economists propose such a mechanism. Rather, workers can buy shares of stock only in financial markets. Owning stock, by giving a worker a share of a corporation, indirectly allows a worker to own a share of the physical capital owned by the corporation. However, at present it is substantially more expensive to buy a share of stock on the market than to buy the physical capital owned by the corporation. At current stock prices, it costs approximately $1.60 in stock to buy $1.00 of physical capital held by corporations. The market value of outstanding shares of U.S. corporations was $11,490 billion as of December 31, 1997 (Federal Reserve Board, Flow of Fund Accounts, table L213, line 19, available at www.bea.doc.gov). The current value of the tangible assets of U.S. corporations is $7,317.6 billion. This estimate is derived from the Federal Reserve Board Balance Sheets, imputing a growth rate for 1997 that was equal to the rate for 1996. Also, the net debt of U.S. corporations at the end of 1997, approximately $1,000 billion, was subtracted (table B102, line 20 - line 6).

Although the relationship between stock returns and economic growth is not very direct at any point in time, there are some things we can say about the two over a long time horizon, such as the 75-year planning period for Social Security.

The return to holding stock consists of two parts, dividend payouts to shareholders and the increase in the price of the stock. Profits are central to both dividends and share prices. Dividends are paid directly out of profits, and typically firms pay out approximately half of their after-tax profits in dividends. Currently, dividend payouts equal about 1.5 percent of the price of an average share of stock (*ERP* 1999, table B-95). For the dividend payout to rise, either profits have to increase or firms have to spend less in other areas, most importantly investment. The implication is that, unless firms substantially curtail their rate of investment, a move that will slow growth and lower future profits, they will be able to increase dividend payouts only at the rate of growth of profits.[2] Therefore, a reasonable assumption is that, over the long run, dividends grow at the same rate as profits.

It is somewhat more difficult to establish the link between share prices and profits, but some general points hold true. The ratio of share prices to profits has fluctuated enormously through time. In the years since World War II, the ratio of the price of an average share of stock to corporate profits has been as low as 7.4 to 1 (the ratio in 1979). At the other extreme, it reached 28.0 to 1 in the fall of 1998.[3] Given this large range, it is not easy to say what the correct ratio of the share price to corporate earnings should be, but we should expect it to depend in part on expectations of future profit growth and the returns available on alternative assets, such as government bonds. In order to keep the price-to-earnings ratio constant, the share price must grow at exactly the same rate as profits. In other words, if the current record-high price-to-earnings ratios are to be maintained, then stock prices must grow at exactly the same rate as profits. If profits grow 10.0 percent in the next year, then stock prices must also rise 10.0 percent. If stock prices rise more rapidly than

2. A firm can increase dividends by curtailing investment only for so long. At some point, the firm will be paying out all profits in dividends and will have ceased to undertake any net new investment.

3. These numbers are taken from the *Economic Report of the President* (1999, table B-95). They are based on the S&P 500 and average after-tax corporate earnings for the previous four quarters. Other indexes and different measures of profit will give slightly different numbers.

10.0 percent but profits stay at 10.0 percent, then price-to-earnings ratios will rise. If stock prices rise less rapidly than 10.0 percent, then price-to-earnings ratios will fall.

The two points laid out above concerning dividends and price-to-earnings ratios allow us to make a link between the growth rate of profits and the rate of return on stocks. If the price-to-earnings ratio remains constant and the share of profits paid out as dividends remains constant, then the return on a share of stock will be equal to the sum of the growth rate of profits and the dividend-to-price ratio. For example, suppose that profits grow 5.0 percent a year and the ratio of the dividend to the share price is 2.0 percent. The total return for holding a share of stock will be 7.0 percent. The 5.0 percent growth in profits means that the share price will increase by 5.0 percent, assuming that the price-to-earnings ratio stays constant, and the dividend payout will provide an additional 2.0 percentage points of return, bringing the total return to 7.0 percent.

To take a simple example, suppose a share of stock sells for $100 and pays out $2 a year in dividends (roughly the current ratio). If profits rise by 5.0 percent, then the share price will go up by 5.0 percent, or $5, to $105. The total return to the shareholder will then be 7.0 percent (the $2 dividend payout plus the $5 capital gain equals a $7 total return, or 7% of $100).

In this way, these two simple assumptions—that the portion of profits paid out as dividends stays constant and that the price-to-earnings ratio remains constant—allow us to derive a projection of the returns to holding stock from a projection of the rate of growth of profits.

We do not have to go far for a projection of profit growth over the next 75 years: it appears implicitly in the assumed rate of growth of wages and gross domestic product (GDP) in the report of the Social Security trustees. The report assumes that the wage share of GDP does not change over this period, so therefore the profit share of GDP also must not change.[4] If the profit share of GDP does not change, then profits will grow at the same rate as GDP, which the trustees project at 1.5 percent a year. In other words, the projec-

4. This assumption is made explicitly in the *Report of the 1994–96 Advisory Council on Social Security*, vol. 2, *Reports of the Technical Panel on Trends and Issues in Retirement Savings and Presentations to the Council* (Washington, D.C.: U.S. Government Printing Office, 1997.) The term "profit share" is used here for simplicity. The more accurate term would be capital share, referring to profit and net interest payments. The distinction is likely to have little consequence over this long time frame and will be discussed later in this chapter.

tions in the trustees' report imply that corporate profits will grow at an average real rate (adjusted for inflation) of less than 1.5 percent per year over the
next 75 years.

This information, along with our simplifying assumptions, allows us to
make a projection of average stock returns over this period. The assumption
that price-to-earnings ratios remain constant means that, on average, inflation-adjusted stock prices will rise by less than 1.5 percent a year over the
next 75 years. The current dividend payout will add another 2.0 percentage
points to this return, bringing the total return to 3.5 percent, half the yield
generally assumed by the privatizers. Due to compounding, this difference
will have an enormous impact on any calculation of the benefits from a privatized system. Investing $1,000 in the stock market at a 7.0 percent return will
get you $14,974 at the end of 40 years; at a 3.5 percent return, the same $1,000
will get you only $3,959. Privatizing Social Security will not be nearly as much
fun in this scenario.

Is There a Way to Beat 3.5 Percent?

The projected 3.5 percent return depends on a number of simplifying
assumptions, as noted earlier. Perhaps if we changed one of these assumptions, the privatizers' dreams will still be attainable.

To begin with, the price-to-earnings ratio does not have to remain constant. As noted earlier, this ratio has fluctuated enormously through time,
and maybe it will rise enough over this period to sustain the 7.0 percent returns the privatizers are counting on.

While few things are literally impossible, this one has to be close. The
price-to-earnings ratio can certainly rise for 1 or 2 years, or even 5 or 10, but
stretching this out over 20, 30, or 50 years yields numbers that can scare even
a privatizer. Figure 5-1 illustrates the average price-to-earnings ratios that
would result in the years 2015, 2035, 2055, and 2075 assuming 6.0 percent,
7.0 percent, and 8.0 percent average real returns over this period.[5] Since the
current price-to-earnings ratio is already at or near a record high, even those

---

5. If profits grow only at the same rate as the economy, and dividends grow only at the
same rate as profits, then in order to get a rate of return greater than the sum of the economy's
growth rate (the trustees assume 1.5 percent) and the dividend payout rate (currently 2.0
percent), the dividend payout must fall each year relative to the stock price. Maintaining
this rate of return will require each year that even more of the return must come from a rise
in the stock price, pushing up the price-to-earnings ratio even faster.

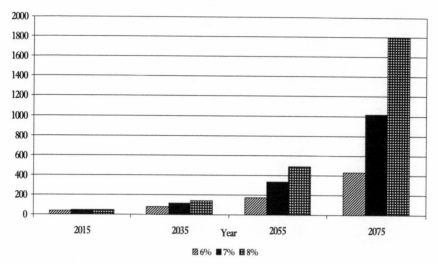

Figure 5-1. Projected Price-to-Earnings Ratios Under Three Profit-Rate Scenarios

for 2015 are way beyond any previously seen in the U.S. stock market. If the average return in the stock market is just 6.0 percent over this period, then the price-to-earnings ratio will rise to 38 to 1; the privatizers' preferred 7.0 percent rate of return will push it to 45 to 1. By 2035, the numbers are even more incredible. The price-to-earnings ratio will be 77 to 1 under a 6.0 return and 117 to 1 under a 7.0 percent return. By the end of the 75-year planning horizon, the privatizers will need a 1070 to 1 price-to-earnings ratio; the optimists who expect 8.0 percent returns are counting on a ratio of 1800 to 1.

It is possible to change some of the other assumptions in this analysis. For instance, maybe the trustees are wrong and the profit share of income will actually rise through this period. The profit share has actually fluctuated a fair amount over the last 50 years, and there is no reason it cannot change in the future. But there are two problems with proceeding along this route. First, the profit share of corporate income, now at 17.2 percent of GDP, is already high; by comparison, it averaged 14.6 percent from 1959 to 1997. The fact that the profit share is so high relative to its long-term average suggests that it may be more likely to go down than up.

The second problem with assuming that the profit share will rise enough to boost stock returns is that such growth implies that wages will go through the floor. If the profit share rises, then the wage share must fall. So if the trustees' growth projections are correct, then the wage share will have to fall enormously throughout this period in order to allow profits to rise enough to yield the returns promised by the privatizers. For example, to maintain an average real return of 7.0 percent, by 2015 wages will have to be 45 percent lower than the trustees' projections assume. Even a 6.0 percent return requires a reduction in wages of 33 percent compared to the baseline projections in the trustees' report. By 2035, in the 7.0 percent scenario, wages would have to be negative.

Other assumptions in this scenario can be changed, but none of them can make a big difference in the basic picture.[6] In summary, it is unrealistic to

6. The other assumptions that could be changed include: (1) the dividend-to-profits ratio can rise; (2) the share of interest in capital income can fall, leaving higher profits to pay out to shareholders; (3) the corporate sector can expand relative to the economy as a whole, allowing profits to rise more rapidly in this sector than in the economy as a whole; and (4) the profits of U.S. corporations can rise more rapidly than domestic profits due to substantial investments abroad. Let's take each of these points in turn.

The dividend-to-profits ratio could double to 4.0 percent if all profits were paid out as dividends. A small portion of this increase could come about by eliminating net purchases of stock in the corporate sector, thereby raising the amount of money paid out in dividends by $41.2 billion in 1997 (Flow of Fund Accounts, table F213, line 1, available at www.bog.frb.fed.us). This move would raise the dividend payout ratio by 0.36 percentage points to 2.36 percent. If the dividend payout ratio were raised further by cutting the rate of investment, the growth rate of the economy would fall below the projections in the trustees' report. Thus, profits (and wages) would grow less rapidly than projected. In this case, the price-to-earnings ratio would still have to soar to provide the returns promised by the privatizers, but wage growth would be minimal over this period.

As for the share of interest in capital income, interest payments currently are a relatively small portion of capital income. In 1997, they were 18.3 percent, well below the average of 21.1 percent over the period from 1959 to 1997 (National Income and Product Accounts, table 116, lines 9 and 17, available at www.bea.doc.gov). Also, interest payments, unlike profits, are not subject to the corporate income tax, meaning that even if interest payments went to zero, after-tax profits would rise by only 22 percent. Over a 20-year period, this rate of increase could allow profits to grow by roughly 1.0 percentage point a year more rapidly than in the base case. Since interest payments will not go to zero (corporations continue to borrow, and the interest rate is already low compared to the levels of the last 25 years), a switch from interest income to profit income will not change the basic story.

As for expansion of the corporate sector, this sector currently makes up about 60.6 percent of the economy. There has been no clear trend in the growth of the corporate sector relative to the economy as a whole over the postwar years, but the level hit in 1997 was the highest attained during this period. Since it is already such a large share of GDP, even a small difference in growth rates would soon eliminate the nonprofit sector, the government sector, and the unincorporated business sector. For example, if the growth rate of the corporate sector exceeded the growth rate of the economy by 1.0 percentage point, the rest of the

assume stock returns that are anywhere close to those used by the privatizers in their calculations of the benefits of a privatized system. In fact, even the 3.5 percent average return noted above may prove too optimistic. The current price-to-earnings ratio is at or near its highest point in the postwar period, and the profit share of corporate income is close to its highest point in the last 50 years (exceeded only by the peak profit years at the beginning of the Vietnam War). The before-tax profit rate is similarly near postwar highs, and the after-tax profit rate is at a postwar high (see Poterba 1997 and Baker 1996). If any, or all, of these numbers revert back to their long-period average, then the stock market can be expected to give returns that are even lower than 3.5 percent, at least for the period of time that the decline is occurring.

For example, if the profit share of corporate GDP fell back to its long-term average over the next 20 years, then the rate of growth of profits would be 1.2 percent annually. Combining this growth with the assumption of a constant share of profits paid out as dividends and a constant price-to-earnings ratio gives an average return of just 3.2 percent annually. In fact, the Congressional Budget Office projects exactly this sort of trend in profits over the next 10 years. It expects profits to fall in constant dollars over this period, so that by 2008 they will be 5.0 percent lower than in 1998. In this case, the above assumptions would imply a real return on stock of 1.5 percent over the next 10 years.

---

economy will have disappeared in the year 2050. Therefore, the extent to which growth in the corporate sector exceeds growth in the overall economy will not affect the profit projections discussed here.

As for the last point, while U.S. firms are investing substantial amounts abroad, foreign firms are also investing substantial amounts in the U.S. economy, meaning that some of the profits generated in the U.S. economy have been going to foreign firms. To date, these trends have been largely offsetting. The ratio of the net foreign profits of U.S. corporations to domestically generated capital income (National Income and Product Accounts, table 1.14, line 20, minus table 1.16, line 9, divided by table 1.16, line 9 plus line 7) was 10.2 percent in 1997, compared to 14.2 percent in 1988, the last business cycle peak. There would have to be an enormous increase in U.S. investment in developing nations, all of which paid off, to substantially affect this picture.

One last point is worth noting. It is possible that people in the United States could purchase stocks in rapidly growing developing nations. This analysis provides no insight into the expected returns in this situation, but the prospect of investing in stock markets in Mexico, China, or Indonesia would have to be viewed as substantially more risky than investing in the U.S. stock market or in those of other developed nations.

If the price-to-earnings ratio falls back to its long-period average of 14.4 percent, then the prospects for stockholders could be even worse. If this decline happens over the next 20 years, the average return over the period would be 1.0 percent. If both the price-to-earnings ratio and the profit share of corporate GDP fall back to their long-period average over this period, then the average annual returns to stockholders would be 0.8 percent.

A drop in the price-to-earnings ratio is exactly what has to happen if returns in the stock market are to equal their long-period averages in the context of extremely slow growth. When the price-to-earnings ratio falls, stockholders are paying less for each dollar in dividends, which means that dividends make up a larger portion of the return. When growth is slow, the dividend-to-price ratio has to be much higher in order to sustain a high total return. For example, if the price-to-earnings ratio fell to half its current level, the dividend-to-price ratio would rise from 2.0 percent to 4.0 percent, allowing for a return of 5.5 percent in the context of 1.5 percent annual growth. If real returns on the order of 6.0–7.0 percent are to be sustained in the context of growth averaging less than 1.5 percent annually, then the price-to-earnings ratio will have to fall to less than half its current level.

This is one of the great ironies of the drive for privatization. The major factor behind public enthusiasm for privatization has been the long boom in the stock market. However, this boom has driven price-to-earnings ratios to a level at which it is impossible to project high returns into the future. The only way to sustain high stock returns in the low-growth economy projected by the trustees is for the stock market to plunge, leading to far lower price-to-earnings ratios and therefore much higher dividend-to-price ratios. However, this sort of crash in the stock market is likely to dampen enthusiasm for privatization considerably.

Before dropping this discussion of prospective returns there is one other negative scenario worth noting. The privatizers often use the "high-cost" scenario in the Social Security trustees' report to make their case that Social Security is in big trouble. As was noted in chapter 1, even the intermediate-cost scenario involves pessimistic assumptions about the future, so the high-cost scenario seems extraordinarily dire. But if the high-cost scenario proves to be closer to the mark, then other things will be affected besides Social Security. For example, the growth rate of profits will be only 0.9 percent for the next 75 years, lower than the 1.5 percent projected in the trustees' report. As a result, the average annual rate of return on stocks, using the same assumptions as above, will be 2.9 percent. Thus, the high-cost scenario may make Social Security appear to have bigger problems, but it also makes privatization less attractive as an alternative.

The Returns from Privatization: Going Down from 3.5 Percent

Adjusting the assumed returns on stocks to make them correspond with the projections for GDP growth in the trustees' report goes far toward deflating the privatizers' rosy scenario, but it is only part of the story. There are several other factors that we must take into consideration before getting an accurate assessment of the returns we can expect in a privatized system. First, most people will typically hold a mix of assets, not just stocks, through their working careers; these other assets might provide a lower rate of return but will be less risky than stocks. Second, the proposed mandated savings program will carry significant administrative costs. Third, additional tax increases will be required to finance the transition to a privatized system, and these must be factored into any calculation of rates of return. Finally, there is the question of how assets are drawn down when a worker retires. If workers want to buy an annuity that provides them with a guaranteed income throughout their retirement, as Social Security provides now, the private market must incur a substantial cost.

It is standard in assessing privatization proposals to assume that individuals will hold a mix of assets of 50 percent stocks and 50 percent bonds (see, e.g., Advisory Council 1997 and EBRI 1998a), thereby lowering the rate of return on a personal savings account below the projected 3.5 rate of return on stocks in the best of the scenarios described above.[7] The trustees project that the average real rate of return on government bonds will be 2.8 percent over the next 75 years, so if an individual holds half of his or her assets in stock and half in bonds, the average return will be 3.15 percent.

The next issue is the cost of administering individual accounts. There is a considerable range of uncertainty here, since the actual costs will depend to a large extent on how closely the system is regulated. In a tightly regulated system, which offers individuals few choices between plans, the costs may be relatively low. The best plans in the private sector, such as TIAA-CREF, the

---

7. In some of the scenarios described above the return on stocks was lower than the projected return on bonds. In these cases, holding a portion of assets in bonds will raise the average rate of return.

retirement plan for many college and university faculty and staff, have administrative costs of approximately 0.4 percent of assets, but the costs in most plans are considerably higher. A recent study reported in the February 1996 issue of *Plan Sponsor* magazine found that the expense ratios for 401(k) plans holding mutual funds concentrated in equities average 1.44 percent a year. A study of actively managed pension funds in the early 1990s found that average administrative costs were 1.0–1.5 percent annually (Lakonishok, Shleifer, and Vishny 1992). In addition, the funds ran up substantial turnover costs due to frequent stock trading. On average, after deducting these costs, the funds examined gave net returns that were 1.0 percentage points less than a portfolio based on holding the S&P 500 index. In the retail market for mutual funds it is common to find administrative costs well in excess of 1.0 percent a year.[8] Moreover, some funds charge substantial "loads," or fees upon deposit, and "redemption fees," assessed at the time money is pulled out of the account. It is also important to note that the cost of trading stock—the bid-ask spread and any brokers' commissions incurred by the fund—is not included in these expense ratios. Finally, these expense numbers do not include the regulatory costs of holding these funds subject to the favored tax treatment of 401(k) plans.

In an unregulated or loosely regulated system, there are likely to be substantial differences in administrative costs across the income spectrum. High-wage workers, who have substantial amounts to put aside, are likely to see relatively low costs, since firms will be anxious to have their business. In many cases these workers will already have some sort of 401(k) plan or mutual fund, to which the new mandated account might be simply appended. Low-wage workers are likely to receive much less favorable treatment. The costs of administering an account are largely independent of the amount of money in the account, meaning that the administrative expenses for accounts of low-wage workers will be a much higher percentage of their holdings. Low-wage workers also change jobs far more frequently than do high-wage workers, and they often spend significant periods of time outside the labor force. Take a low-wage worker who works part of the year, or part-time, and earns $5,000 a year. The minimum 5.0 percent investment required by most privatization

8. *Fortune* magazine lists the expense ratios for the "best funds" every quarter. The stock funds in this list have expense ratios averaging close to 1.0 percent; some have expense ratios that are considerably higher.

Chapter Five

proposals would come to $250 a year; it is unlikely that Wall Street firms will actively compete for such small sums. Unless the system is tightly regulated, such workers are likely to be gouged with privatization. Annual administrative expenses in excess of 3.0 or even 5.0 percent a year could make their net annual returns negative.[9]

If the system of mandated savings is unregulated or loosely regulated, low-wage workers will probably be treated the same as they are now by the financial system: badly. Many poor neighborhoods have few or no banks, and banks now charge substantial fees for checking accounts with low balances. Partly as a result, 17.0 percent of the population does not even have a checking account. Their "banks" tend to be check-cashing outlets, which often charge fees of 1–2 percent for the service. There is little reason to expect that low-wage earners will be treated any better by the financial system under a regime of mandated savings.

Perhaps a mandated savings system will be instituted with substantial regulation. The federal government may set a tight limit on the number of competing firms, thereby ensuring that each firm has a large share of the market and allowing regulators to scrutinize investment behavior to guard against unreasonable risks. The government can also allow closer scrutiny of marketing practices to prevent deceptive or even fraudulent sales pitches, and it could mandate a strictly regulated fee structure, in which higher-than-market fees on high-wage earners subsidized lower-than-market fees for low-wage earners. It is not clear that the financial industry would allow such regulation—its lobbyists could be expected to fight it intensely—but regulation of this sort might keep administrative fees low.[10]

The president's Advisory Council on Social Security, which assumed that an effective regulatory structure would be established, estimated that the administrative charges on these accounts would be 1.0 percent annually. In this

9. A recent study that examined annual expenses per worker in pension plans run by small companies found that the average administrative costs for defined-contribution plans were $259 per worker per year (Mitchell 1996, table 14). If expenses of this magnitude were assessed against each worker's account, low-wage workers would earn negative rates of return.

10. One factor that might lead to intense lobbying is that banks and brokerage houses might have difficulty explaining to their customers why their fees are so much lower on the mandated savings accounts than on other accounts they offer. In other words, low fees on mandated accounts could end up costing firms tens of billions of dollars annually on the fees charged on existing accounts.

The Glories of Privatization

case, a 1.0 percent annual fee will lower the average rate of return on a mixed stock-bond account to 2.15 percent. At this rate, a $1,000 investment will grow to $2,342 at the end of 40 years, hardly enough to make a worker rich. And there are even more caveats to consider.

If 5.0 percentage points of a worker's payroll taxes are placed in mandated savings accounts and not into Social Security, then this money is not going to the government. The immediate impact is a loss of revenue of approximately $180 billion that has to be offset in some manner. The government could opt to run a deficit of this magnitude, but this is not likely in the current political environment, nor is it a policy typically advocated by supporters of privatization. The loss could be offset by spending cuts, but this would not be an easy task either. Excluding Social Security benefits (even most privatizers acknowledge the need to continue paying promised Social Security benefits to those who have already retired or who are within 5 or 10 years of retirement) and interest on the debt as sources of cuts leaves just $1,090 billion from which to get $180 billion in lost revenue. Since the nation has been through a decade of budget cutting to eliminate the deficit, it is not likely that cuts of this magnitude—16.5 percent of available spending—can be easily found. Furthermore, if the privatizers advocate this route, then they should specify their intended cuts so the public and policymakers can effectively analyze the full cost of their plan. None of the prominent proponents of privatization has yet laid out an agenda in this manner.

In the absence of specified budget cuts, the most reasonable assumption is that the lost revenue will be made up in new taxes. In other words, taxes will have to be raised by an amount approximately equal to 5.0 percentage points of payroll. This amount will gradually fall through time, as the current generation of retired or soon-to-be-retired workers dies and younger workers who are less dependent on Social Security benefits take their place. However, this additional tax, needed to finance the transition, must be included in any full evaluation of rates of return.

The exact size of the transition tax will depend on the period of time over which the transition is funded and how quickly the current schedule of Social Security benefits is phased out. The Employee Benefit Research Institute estimated that the transition tax would be the equivalent of 4.0 percentage points of payroll over a 40-year period (EBRI 1998b, 2).

From the standpoint of calculating rates of return, this is money that is effectively tossed in the trash, since it yields zero return for the worker who pays it. For example, a worker might get a $21.50 return (2.15 percent) on the $1,000 placed in a mandated account this year, but as a result of the privatization tax that worker will be forced to pay an additional $800 that he or she will never see again. This means that the $1,800 paid by the worker this year will leave the worker with $1021.50 next year, a return of negative 43.25 percent.

This calculation understates the true return from a privatized system, since most plans also call for a minimal sub-poverty-level benefit to be provided by the remaining 5.7 percentage points of the payroll tax. This benefit will provide a small positive return, which will raise the average return under privatization for all required payments but still leave the total negative.[11]

However, what is more important than calculating the exact rate of return from privatization plans is recognizing the nature of the deception in the calculations regularly put forward by their proponents. These plans all require a substantial tax increase to finance the transition. However, the additional money assessed to workers through these taxes is not included in the base of the rate-of-return calculation. In other words, the privatizers highlight (and overstate) the return on the money going into the mandated accounts, but they completely ignore the large amounts of money that will have to be paid from another pocket to support the transition. Any honest calculation must include all taxes and payments associated with the proposal. By comparison, the calculations of projected rates of return for Social Security include projected increases in taxes and cuts in benefits.

We have not yet considered the cost of annuities. Most people, when they choose to retire, are going to want some guarantee of an income stream that will last them throughout their retirement. If they simply spend down their savings at a fixed rate, they run the risk of underestimating their life span and ending up without any money left. To avoid this problem, most people would likely purchase an annuity, which provides them with a fixed payment as long as they live. Ideally, they would get a real-valued annuity, a payment that is adjusted for inflation, thereby guaranteeing them a certain living standard throughout their remaining years.

All Social Security payments are in the form of real-valued annuities, but these financial instruments are hard to obtain, and are expensive, in the pri-

11. The Employee Benefit Research Institute calculated that the average payback ratio for a man born in 1976 will be 66 percent under the privatization proposal it modeled. For a woman born in 1976 it estimated a payback ratio of 75 percent (EBRI 1998a, 13).

vate market. The introduction of inflation-adjusted government bonds in 1997, however, allows firms to avoid inflation risk and will presumably lead more firms to offer real-valued annuities in the near future. But even if they become more widely available, they are likely to still be expensive. When they issue annuities, insurance companies and other financial institutions must both cover their expenses and protect themselves against the possibility of adverse selection (i.e., signing up a disproportionate number of people who ultimately have longer-than-average life spans). As a result, insurance companies charge substantial premiums when they issue annuities, and on average workers will get monthly benefits that are considerably less than what they could expect if these benefits were based exclusively on their life expectancy.

A recent study of the premiums assessed on annuities found that insurance companies charge an average of 15–20 percent (Mitchell, Poterba, and Warshawsky 1997), meaning that the retirement income individuals can expect will be 15–20 percent less than they should be able to expect based on their lifetime accumulations. Thus, a worker who has put aside $1,000 every year for 40 years and received a 3.15 percent return before deducting expenses (2.15 percent return after deducting expenses) will have accumulated approximately $63,750. If this worker buys an annuity with this money, he or she will lose between $9,563 and $12,750. If the worker has a life expectancy at age 65 of 19 years (the approximate life expectancy in the year 2040), then he or she can expect an annual payment of between $3,319 and $3,527, or a monthly payment between $277 and $294,[12] not sufficient to provide for much high living.

This sum does not include the sub-poverty-level benefit of roughly $5,000 a year that most plans also provide for virtually all workers. However, the final tally also does not include the additional taxes that workers will be forced to pay to finance the cost of transition. It is also important to remember that this is in many ways an optimistic view of the outcome of privatization. It assumes that the stock market maintains its current record-high price-to-earnings ratios and that the profit share of corporate income remains near its postwar high. It also assumes that Congress legislates effective regulation of the system to keep administrative costs relatively low and minimize fraud.

12. These figures assume a real return of 2.5 percent on the annuity.

Chapter Five

A Modicum of Privatization

Proposals by proponents of privatizing Social Security depend on extremely unlikely scenarios and misleading methods of measurement. Their projections of future stock market returns are impossibly optimistic, and they ignore the impact of administrative costs and the tax burden that will have to be imposed to finance the transition. But if the purpose of the mandated accounts is to allow workers to receive the benefit of high expected returns in the stock market, then this goal can be achieved far more efficiently within the current system. The Social Security trust fund could be partially invested in the stock market, as was suggested in the plan put forward by former Social Security Commissioner Robert Ball and supported by five other members of the president's Advisory Council on Social Security. Compared to the mandated savings proposals, which require both a private structure to bring about this outcome and a government regulatory structure to oversee it, this proposal would allow enormous administrative savings. Since the privatization proponents want to preserve the Survivors and Disability Insurance portions of Social Security as well as provide for some minimal benefit for all retirees, it will be necessary to keep the existing bureaucracy in place. This means that the administrative structures needed to run the private system will be a pure waste from a social standpoint. Using the Chilean system as a model, it appears that the costs will be large, perhaps as much as \$30–45 billion annually, given the current size of the program. This is a considerable sum to throw away just to reduce the government's role in securing retirement income.

Opponents of direct government investment of the Social Security trust fund often raise concerns about political interference in investment decisions. Regardless of the validity of such concerns, this problem arises with any type of government-mandated savings, including the privatization plans discussed earlier. The government will always be responsible for regulating the types of investments that can be made with these savings. It is plausible that, just as political factors affect the restrictions that the government applies to money it directly invests, they will also affect mandated savings accounts.

6 | The Advisory Council's Recommendations and Other Fixes

A NUMBER OF PROPOSALS, driven primarily by politics and a high degree of public misunderstanding of the basic facts, are now on the table to reform or otherwise fix Social Security. The problem they all intend to remedy, either by cutting benefits or by privatizing the system, is the small projected shortfall over the 75-year planning period, the gap in terms of percentage of payroll between revenues and obligations. The Social Security trustees peg the amount at 2.07 percent of payroll, split between the employer and the employee (SSA 1999, 3).

The margin of error for projections 75 years into the future is enormous. Compare it to the continual national surprises over the federal budget: economists have been unable to estimate the deficit or surplus within a margin of 80 percent. With that kind of track record, it is questionable whether we should accord a project shortfall of 2.07 percent of payroll over three-quarters of a century any significance at all, especially since the shortfall does not appear until over 30 years from now. In other words, the projected shortfall could easily be within the margin of error for such a forecast, in which case we would have no basis to assert that a shortfall is any more likely than a surplus over the 75-year planning period.

Many of those who would like to preserve Social Security have abandoned the effort to defend the system on the basis of the facts. Their reasoning is as follows. The public believes that Social Security is headed for a crisis when the baby boomers retire. Therefore, we cannot deny this belief without becoming marginalized in the debate. In a political climate driven by focus groups and polling data, it does not take long for the truth to be turned upside down and a consensus to be formed around a whole new reality. When this happens, they say, it is best to join in the new consensus and propose your own plan for solving the problem.

There are, of course, problems with this "truth by focus group" approach. For instance, polling data show that a majority of Americans do not know that electrons are smaller than atoms (*New York Times* 1988). The diffusion of knowledge would be greatly impeded if science teachers were expected to adjust their ideas accordingly. Moreover, recent history suggests that such an approach can be politically self-defeating. Conservatives hammered for years on the idea that welfare perpetuated and even caused poverty, in spite of the overwhelming empirical evidence to the contrary. Those who wanted to preserve the Aid to Families with Dependent Children program (AFDC) as a federal entitlement grew tired of challenging these misconceptions and came to accept the argument that the welfare system needed "reform." Their idea of reform, of course, was different from that of their conservative opponents: they wanted child care, health care, job training, and, most important, access to employment that paid enough to lift a family formerly receiving welfare out of poverty. But accepting the basic premise of welfare's opponents—that welfare was a cause, rather than a result, of poverty—proved to be more costly than they had anticipated. Within a couple of years President Clinton had signed a bill abolishing what had been, at least since the 1960s, a major federal entitlement for poor children.

In the case of Social Security, it would be even more of a mistake to accept the premises of the reformers, because these premises are so easily shown to be false. There are no complex relationships of cause and effect to be extracted from empirical evidence, relationships that open the door for anyone with access to the op-ed pages to argue his or her case and decorate it with colorful anecdotes. As we have seen, the case for Social Security's "looming insolvency" is constructed around a handful of verbal and accounting tricks, with a few demographic facts taken deceptively out of context.

The dangers of capitulating to a false consensus around the state of Social Security can be seen in the proposals that have been getting the most serious consideration so far: they involve regressive benefit cuts, generally hitting poor retirees the hardest, and various forms of privatization.

Three Ideas from the Advisory Council

Every four years the secretary of Health and Human Services is required to appoint the Advisory Council on Social Security to review the status of the program and that of other federal entitlements. The most recent advisory

The Advisory Council's Recommendations

council released its report in January 1997. Although the council was unable to agree upon a unified proposal, the three plans put forth by its factions have already shown themselves to be a formative part of the debate.

The most radical of the advisory council's plans, supported by 5 of its 13 members, calls for diverting almost half of the Social Security payroll tax (5.0 percentage points) to personal security accounts (PSAs). But the tax increase required by such a shift would guarantee negative returns on Social Security payments for the employees of the next few decades. To make matters worse, returns from the accounts would not, for most recipients, significantly surpass those of the current system. Finally, the enormous administrative complexities and waste involved in regulating and maintaining such a system of private accounts also turn out to be quite formidable. (These issues are discussed in detail in chapter 5.)

Two other members of the council, including the chairman, Edward Gramlich (now on the Board of Governors of the Federal Reserve), proposed a "mini-privatization" plan calling for individual accounts (IAs); this plan would add a tax of 1.6 percent of payroll designated for privatized accumulations. Since this amounts to less than $400 a year for the average employee, many workers would probably not find it worth the effort to investigate the various choices for investment. The main purpose of this small-scale privatization seems to be to raise the payroll tax in a way that will be more politically palatable than an ordinary tax hike.

Both of the privatization plans, whose proponents together represented a majority of the 13-member advisory council, advocated raising the retirement age. This measure has widespread support among policy analysts, who argue that, as life expectancy increases, so should Social Security's "normal retirement age," now set at 65. At first glance this seems like a reasonable argument, but when we take into account the large disparities in life expectancy between various demographic groups, the argument begins to break down. A typical black male worker who is 39 years old today can expect about 2.3 years of full retirement benefits, compared with 8.4 years for a white male of the same cohort (CDCP/NCHS 1993). Thus, the impact of raising the retirement age will be much more drastic for African Americans than for whites.

Although most Americans are not aware of it, Social Security's normal retirement age was already raised in 1983. Those born after 1943 will not be able to retire with full benefits until age 66; for those born after 1959 the retirement age was increased to 67. The disproportionate impact of this change is already severe: for the 39-year-old black male worker, it has cut nearly half of his retirement years, compared with less than a fifth for a white male worker.[1] The PSA and IA plans propose to speed up the implementation of this increase and then raise the retirement age over time to 70 years. The PSA plan also proposes to raise the early-retirement age from 62 to 65.

Although some have argued that they expect the racial differences in life expectancy to abate in the twenty-first century, it would be more prudent to wait until such trends actually appear before legislating these kinds of benefit cuts. The ratio of black to white male life expectancy, for example, is the same today as it was 50 years ago (CDCP/NCHS 1997).

These differential impacts apply not only to racial groups but to income groups as well. Although the U.S. government does not collect mortality statistics by class—that is, by income, education, or occupation—there is considerable evidence that most of the racial differences in U.S. mortality data are attributable to class differences (for a review, see Navarro 1990). For example, the difference in life expectancy between low- and high-income groups of 25-year-old males was found to be about 23 percent, even greater than the 16.2 percent white-black differential (Rogot, Sorlie, and Johnson 1992; CDCP/NCHS 1993). We would therefore expect similarly severe and disproportionate effects on low-income and blue-collar workers from raising the retirement age.

The fact that many beneficiaries select early retirement between the ages of 62 and 64 does not change the results. Benefits under early retirement are lower: workers retiring at 62 will receive 80 percent of the benefits they would have received if they retired at 65. This reduction, which remains in effect for the rest of the beneficiary's retirement, is calculated so that, on average, the retiree will receive the same amount of benefits over the rest of his or her life. Early-retirement benefits at age 62 will thus be reduced to 75 percent of full benefits when the normal retirement age increases to 66 and to 70 percent when it hits 67, with similar reductions if the normal retirement age were increased to 70. As these changes are phased in, they will have a significant

1. These differences would be less pronounced if we were to look at, for example, life expectancies for those who survive to age 65. We consider life expectancy at age 39 here because that is the cohort first affected by the increase in the retirement age to 67, and by this age the typical worker has already paid taxes into the system for nearly half of his or her working life.

regressive impact on the income distribution of the elderly, since any across-the-board cuts hurt poorer beneficiaries more than those in the upper-income brackets. The bottom 20 percent of Social Security recipients depend on the program for 81 percent of their income, compared to 23 percent for the top 20 percent.

The trend toward declining job security for older workers raises other concerns about increasing the retirement age at this time. Over the last decade and a half there has been a significant increase in displacement rates for older workers, often through downsizing. For men aged 55–64, the median length of job tenure has declined from 15.3 years in 1986 to 10.5 years in 1998 (BLS 1998a). Unless these trends are reversed, we can expect that many workers who are forced to work into their late sixties will not be doing the jobs they attained at the peak of their careers but instead something much lower on the pay scale.

Many policy analysts cannot understand what it is like to approach retirement from a job that is not all that interesting or that has taken its toll on a body that is not even 60 years old—as is the case in many blue-collar jobs. The professors and pundits who advocate increasing the retirement age probably like their jobs, and they may find increasing enjoyment in their work into their late sixties or even seventies. But this is not the situation faced by everyone else.

As life expectancy increases, a time will come when the electorate will have to decide how much of its longer life span it wants to spend in retirement. A choice for longer retirement spans will require higher taxes. This decision does not necessarily imply a reduced standard of living, since productivity also increases each year: it has increased 50 percent over the last 30 years (*ERP* 1999). But a choice must be made about how much of these productivity gains should be spent on years of retirement. It is possible to imagine a rational and informed policy debate over this important social choice, but the present efforts to cut benefits on the basis of widespread misinformation are not that kind of debate.

Investing the Trust Fund

As noted above, the Advisory Council on Social Security divided into three factions. The two that included privatization within their plans—the members favoring PSAs and IAs—also called for raising the retirement age. These two groups accounted for 7 of the 13 members of the council.

The remaining 6 members formed the maintenance-of-benefits group, which, unlike the others, did not support any privatization or increases in the retirement age. This group did, however, propose investing part of the Social Security trust fund in private stocks and bonds, but this is not the same as a system of individual private accounts, because Social Security would remain a defined-benefit program. The trust fund, not individual beneficiaries, would invest a portion of the accumulated surplus and bear the risk of any decline in stock prices. Furthermore, this plan would avoid the substantial administrative and regulatory costs of individual accounts. The portion of the trust fund invested in the stock market would simply be placed in an index fund, thereby avoiding such complications as influencing the stock values of individual companies.

Those who advocate investing part of the trust fund in stocks argue that this move will help shore up Social Security's finances. However, this argument is based on the assumption that equities will provide a 7 percent real rate of return over the 75-year planning period. As explained in chapter 5, this rate of return is not possible, given the slow (1.5 percent per year) growth assumed by Social Security's actuaries. When we substitute more realistic returns (about 3.5 percent) consistent with the actuaries' growth projections, it becomes apparent that there is little to be gained by investing the trust fund in equities. (Of course, if the economy were to grow fast enough to provide a 7 percent rate of return, the Social Security trust fund would pile up an enormous surplus indefinitely—without having to invest anything in stocks).

There are also political disadvantages to giving the trust fund a sizable stake in the stock market. Most importantly, the proposal to invest the trust fund in stocks could help open the door to real privatization—that is, the diversion of Social Security revenues to individual accounts—which would undermine the stability and security of the program's guaranteed benefits. Ironically, the New Deal legislation that established Social Security required that any surplus be invested only in U.S. Treasury obligations, partly because of the business community's fears that stock holdings would be leveraged to press for increases in corporate accountability. Six decades later, that fear has not completely disappeared: Wall Street still opposes the trust fund's investment in the stock market (Weinstein 1998). But whatever the political consequences, such investments by themselves would not seem likely to have much effect on the future of Social Security.

Other Regressive Cuts

While raising the retirement age would be toughest for low-income and African American men, another cut proposed by the advisory council would hit women the hardest. This cut, which would also disproportionately hurt low-income workers, was supported by a majority of the council, including the maintenance-of-benefits group.

The proposed cut would change the way benefits are computed. Currently, benefits are based on the earnings record of the employee from age 22 through 61.[2] Social Security computes the benefit on the basis of the employee's best 35 years—that is, those of highest earnings.[3] The council proposal would add three years to this computation, so that it would be based on 38 years. The first problem with this change is that women spend a lot more time, on average, out of the labor force than do men; approximately 75 percent of men, but only 25 percent of women, have 35 or more years of covered earnings.[4] As a result, most women beneficiaries would have 3 years of zero earnings added to the computation of their benefits. The second problem with a change of this sort results from the progressive structure of Social Security's benefit formula. For the first $505 of average monthly earnings, the employee gets 90 percent in benefits. For the next $2,538, he or she receives 32 percent, then 15 percent of further income up to the maximum taxable earnings ($72,600 in 1999). This progressive payout schedule counteracts the harsh regressiveness of the payroll tax, allowing the program to have a net effect on income distribution that is progressive. But it also means that any reduction of the calculated earnings on which benefits are based will affect low-income workers much more than those who are better off. Adding a year of zero wages knocks down that earnings base, and every dollar knocked off this base means 90

2. Earnings after age 61 or before age 22 can be used in place of the years from 22 to 61 if this would result in a higher benefit (see SSA 1996b, 56).

3. Earnings for each year (prior to age 61) are multiplied by an indexing factor that is based on the average wage in the economy at the time. Annual earnings above a certain maximum ($72,600 for 1999) are not subject to the Social Security payroll tax and are therefore not included in the calculation of benefits.

4. Data from Office of the Actuary, Social Security Administration. Research by Iams (1993) shows comparable results for married women, at least for the first several years of cohorts that would be affected by the increased computational period. Covered earnings refer to earnings that are subject to the Social Security payroll tax.

Chapter Six

cents taken from a low-income earner versus 15 cents taken from a high-income earner.

Table 6-1 illustrates the sum of these two effects on the benefits of various employees.[5] The gender effect can be seen by comparing the typical female worker who retires on the basis of her own work record with the typical male beneficiary. The average benefit for the female worker—$621 per month under current rules—would drop 4.4 percent, or $328 a year. By comparison, the average male beneficiary would lose about 2.6 percent of his benefits.[6] The hardest hit would be women whose monthly benefits under the current system are $426 or less. A female retiree at this benefit level would lose 7.9 percent of her benefits, $403 a year.[7] Retirees who earned the maximum taxable income throughout their working lives would lose only 1.2 percent of benefits.[8] The percentage loss suffered by low-benefit female retirees is thus more than six times that of the highest earnings group.[9]

The regressiveness of this change is compounded by the fact that poor and low-income retirees are overwhelmingly more dependent on Social Security income than those who are better off. For example, the median income of an individual poor person 65 or older was $5,427 in 1994. Eighty-three percent of the income of this group, which numbers 2.4 million people, is from Social Security (SSA 1996b, 171). A poor female retiree at this income level who is hit with the full effect of the proposed computational change would lose $358 a year, or 6.6 percent of her annual income. Although current

5. The examples given here are all based on a worker retiring at age 65. Most people retire earlier (i.e., 62–64) with reduced benefits, but they would still suffer the same reduction in their primary insurance amount (i.e., the base from which their reduced benefit is calculated).

6. This effect is estimated under the assumption that the three years of earnings added to the computation of benefits are, on average, half the value of the average indexed earnings of the highest 35 years.

7. The effect on female retirees is computed assuming that the three years added to the computation period are years spent outside the labor force.

8. This effect does not depend on the distribution of earnings over the employee's career, since earnings are assumed to be at or above the maximum taxable earnings for all 38 (or more) years. It results from the fact that the maximum taxable earnings for earlier years, even after indexing, are lower than those for later years (see SSA 1996b, p. 43).

9. A large proportion (probably close to half) of new female retirees are eligible for benefits on the basis of their husbands' earnings; these women's benefits would not be affected by the number of years that they spent out of the labor force.

The Advisory Council's Recommendations

Table 6-1. Benefit Cuts Due to Proposed Change in Computation Period

Retiree	Monthly benefit based on 35-year computation period	Monthly benefit based on 38-year computation period	Change in yearly benefits	Percentage change in benefits
Low benefit female	$ 426	$ 392	−$403	−7.9%
Average benefit female	$ 621	$ 594	−$328	−4.4%
Average benefit male	$ 810	$ 788	−$254	−2.6%
High benefit (maximum taxable earnings)	$1,285	$1,269	−$191	−1.2%

Source: *SSA* 1996b; authors' calculations.

beneficiaries would not be affected, this change would inflict a terrible hardship upon the elderly poor who will retire just a few years from now.

By contrast, employees who earned the maximum taxable income throughout their working lives would lose less than one-quarter of 1 percent of their income.

It is especially difficult to justify a cut that hits elderly women the hardest when so many are already poor. The official poverty rate for women aged 65 or older is 14.9 percent; it is 25.3 percent for elderly women who are not living with family members. The poverty rate of the general population is 12 percent (SSA 1996b, 170–72).[10]

These examples illustrate how benefit cuts that do not appear unconscionable at first glance can significantly worsen poverty and income distribution among the elderly. The combination of Social Security's progressive payout structure with the disproportionate reliance of the poorest elderly on the program's benefits practically guarantees such results. Yet the regressive impact of the advisory council's proposed cuts received almost no attention when the report was released.

On the heels of the advisory council's recommendations, a private group calling itself the National Commission on Retirement Policy issued a report recommending similar, plus deeper and additional, cuts. For example, it called

10. The data are from 1994 (the latest available).

for increasing the benefit computation years from 35 to 40 (instead of the Advisory Council's 38) and a steep cut in the spousal benefit from 50 to 33 percent. It also proposed faster increases in the retirement age, to 70 by 2029, with an increase in the early-retirement age from 62 to 65 by 2017. It also added a different kind of cut, which reduces the payout rate only for middle- to higher-income workers. While the latter does not hit the poorest workers, its effect on the distribution of income among the elderly would still be regressive. In addition, the group proposed a partial privatization plan that would divert 2.0 percentage points (16 percent of the Social Security payroll tax) to mandatory individual accounts.

The plan received considerable and generally favorable treatment in the press. In a front-page story, the *New York Times* described it as "the most comprehensive package of recommendations to date for remaking Social Security in preparation for the baby-boom generation's retirement" and noted that "the report is likely to wield considerable influence at the White House and on Capitol Hill as Democrats and Republicans seek solutions to one of the most politically sensitive issues facing the nation." The *Times* also noted that "the panel had no members drawn from labor unions or other groups that have fought to maintain Social Security as a guaranteed safety net against poverty in old age" (Stevenson 1998a). Indeed, the panel included business executives of corporations with a direct financial interest in privatization, such as Robert Pozen, chief executive officer of Fidelity Investments; Thomas J. McInerney, president of Aetna Retirement Services; and Donald B. Marron, chairman and chief executive officer of Paine Webber Group. The members of Congress, former government officials, and economists on the panel were people who had previously supported, or could be expected to support, a mixture of benefit cuts and privatization.

Proposals for Means-Testing Benefits

For those who insist on cutting Social Security, one way to avoid a regressive impact would be to deny benefits to senior citizens making more than a certain income. Benefits could be reduced along a scale from middle- to upper-income seniors. Some policy analysts and advocates have argued for "means-testing" on the grounds that the government should not pay money to wealthy senior citizens while it cuts programs for poor children.

There are compelling reasons, however, to reject this approach. Most important is the danger that it poses to the program's broad base of political support. One reason it has been so difficult to cut, privatize, or dismantle Social Security is that 43 million beneficiaries receive it. The more that base is reduced, especially by cutting off those senior citizens who have relatively more of a voice in politics, the shakier Social Security's position becomes.

It is not just the absolute numbers that are significant but the nature of the program as well. Social Security is a social insurance program in which retirement benefits are proportional to one's payments into the system. Means-testing would convert the system into a welfare program. And we know from the recent cancellation of the most important federal welfare entitlement, AFDC, how much more difficult it is to defend welfare against political attacks than it is to defend social insurance.

The justification for denying benefits to people who have paid taxes into the system is also questionable. We do not deny interest payments to wealthy owners of U.S. Treasury bonds, for example, and it is difficult to see how the payment of Social Security benefits to rich senior citizens is any less appropriate. Indeed, why single out senior citizens as a group for special treatment in this regard? If we think that the rich are getting too much of the economic pie, then they should all be taxed more—not just the ones who happen to be over 65.

Means-testing would also entail substantial administrative costs, since there would be a considerable incentive for senior citizens to hide their income and assets in order to qualify for benefits. We have already seen some of these costs in the case of Medicaid, which provides means-tested medical insurance for the poor. Seniors are not all that rich as a group: only 7 percent of senior citizens have annual incomes over $75,000 (Census Bureau 1996). The potential savings from means-testing are therefore limited, and from these we must subtract the costs of policing the system. Weighed against the substantial risks of undermining public support for Social Security, it hardly seems worth the gamble.

A Worsening Problem?

The public is often reminded, even by some of Social Security's more prominent defenders, that the problem with Social Security's finances will only get worse as time passes if nothing is done (Kurtz 1998). Ignoring for the moment that no significant problem exists to begin with, there is a sense in which this statement is partially true. An increase in the program's revenue this week would have a larger effect, thanks to compounding, on closing the

Chapter Six

75-year projected shortfall than would the same dollar amount raised 10 or 15 years from now. So, for example, the 2.2 percent of payroll that would be needed to close the gap today would be about 2.8 percent if we were to wait 15 years.

Yet there is no compelling economic reason for raising this revenue (or reducing benefits) sooner rather than later. At its core, the statement that "the problem will only get worse" is merely expressing two obvious facts: first, if we need a certain amount of additional revenue over a fixed period (in this case, 75 years), then any increment not collected this year will have to be added to later years; second, in a market economy, money earns interest. Any earlier savings will accumulate more interest than later savings. It does not follow, however, that more savings earlier is always the best choice.

A college student who is just managing to cover her expenses for rent and food will probably not be persuaded to reduce her current spending in order to begin saving for retirement. She has good reason to believe that her future income will be higher, and that even the larger amount of future savings that would be necessary to match an earlier, originally smaller amount would be less painful to accumulate at a later time. In this case, it is still as true as ever that "the problem" of her retirement "will only get worse" the longer she waits to begin saving. But this does not mean that her decision to postpone saving throughout her college years is short-sighted or foolish. As economists like to describe it, there is a trade-off between present and future consumption, and individual preferences will play a role in determining how that trade-off is resolved.

The trade-offs involved in a social insurance program for retirement are similar. Instead of individual preferences and an individual choice, we have social preferences and a social choice to make. Our national income will be higher 15 years from now by about 28 percent, according to the Social Security trustees' slow-growth (intermediate) projections. If we assume that what people care about is their real after-tax income, then there is no reason why a 2.8 percent tax increase on income that is 28 percent higher should appear more burdensome than a 2.2 percent increase today. In fact the opposite seems much more likely.

The Way to Real Reform

To reform something, according to Webster's dictionary, is "to amend or improve by change of form or removal of faults or abuses." The regressive cuts and privatization proposals currently on the table would not meet this definition, at least for the overwhelming majority of Americans. It is unfortunate that the word "reform" has become attached to a whole smorgasbord of attacks on the nation's largest and most successful antipoverty program.

However, the Social Security system is not without its faults, and some of these could stand to be corrected. Revenue could even be raised in the process in order to reassure those who are nervous about the possibility of a shortfall over three decades from now. For example, Social Security is currently funded by a regressive payroll tax, which begins with the first dollar earned and stops at $72,600 per year. The program's critics are quick to point out that the typical family pays more in payroll taxes to fund Social Security and Medicare than it does in federal income taxes.[11] In view of the increasing inequality of income—over the last decade almost all of the gains from economic growth have gone to the top 5 percent of the income distribution (Freeman 1996)—a case could be made for reducing the regressive burden of these payroll taxes.

The problem could be addressed by raising or lifting the cap on the payroll tax. In the past, the payroll tax was collected on as much as 90 percent of all wages in covered employment; today's ceiling leaves only about 84.5 percent of earnings taxable. We could raise the ceiling until we were back to 90 percent (Ball 1998); doing so would cover about a quarter of the projected 75-year deficit, although it would undoubtedly provoke some backlash among upper-income taxpayers. A more politically palatable option would be to lift the cap on the employer's part of the tax. This would also have the advantage of raising a good deal of revenue without having to increase benefits for the highest salaried people in the country. This move would close nearly half of the long-range financing gap.

Since the real economic problem that threatens the well-being of future generations is not the baby boomers' retirement but rather the worsening distribution of income, a strong case can be made for making the Social Secu-

---

11. The current tax rate for Social Security, or OASDI (Old-Age and Survivors Insurance and Disability Insurance), is 12.4 percent, with half levied on the employee and half on the employer. In this discussion we take the common approach of lumping the OASI (with a tax rate of 10.7 percent) and the DI (1.7 percent) programs together, under the rubric of Social Security. The Medicare program is treated separately; its payroll tax is 2.9 percent, again split between employer and employee. Labor economists customarily treat the employer's part of the payroll tax as being passed on to the employee; hence the sum of Social Security and Medicare payroll taxes comes to 15.3 percent of payroll.

rity system more progressive. This upward redistribution of income has involved not only increasing inequality in wages and salaries but also, in recent years, a shift from labor to nonlabor income (capital gains, dividends, and interest payments). Since 1989, the last business cycle peak, the share of national income going to corporate profits has increased by 3.2 percentage points. If not for this shift, median wage earners would be making $1,100 more per year than they are presently.[12] In view of this shift, it would make sense to supplement Social Security's payroll tax with a tax on nonlabor income. The 1997 budget agreement reduced the top marginal tax rate on capital gains from 28 percent to 20 percent; it fell to 18 percent for assets held more than five years. At the time, Treasury Secretary Robert Rubin correctly noted the general agreement among economists that this tax break was "unlikely to produce much economic benefit" (Bennet 1997). On the contrary, since it enlarges a loophole, it adds waste and inefficiency to the measures taken to shelter other forms of income as capital gains. And it has the rather inequitable result that a wealthy person can sell a fraction of his or her assets and pay a considerably lower tax rate on the billions so earned than a worker pays on his or her annual income over $33,000. We could correct this mistake by restoring the old capital gains tax rate and funneling the difference into the Social Security trust fund. One might object that such a tax would undermine the social insurance character of the system, but such an outcome does not seem likely. The vast bulk of the program's revenues would still come from the payroll tax, and benefits would still be proportional to people's covered earnings.

If the goal is to ensure that Social Security beneficiaries get a share of the record increases in the stock market, as the advocates of privatization claim, there are even simpler ways to achieve it. As economist Robert Eisner (1997) has pointed out, the Treasury could simply pay a higher rate of interest on the funds it borrows from the Social Security trust fund. Raising that rate from 6.3 percent to 9.3 percent would take care of about half of the projected 75-year deficit. Eisner has an even more intuitive solution for the other half: at present, we pay federal income tax on our Social Security taxes, since the latter are not deductible. Why not shift this money from the general revenue to the Social Security trust fund? Since it is a tax on income that goes to

12. Economic Policy Institute analysis of data from the National Income and Product Accounts.

Social Security, it seems reasonable that this "second tax" should go there also.

Other inequities in the system could be ironed out if reform were really the order of the day. As already noted, women are heavily penalized for their time spent out of the workforce, raising children and caring for family members. They also remain concentrated in lower-paying occupations: even today, the median income for female workers full-time, year-round is just under $25,000 (Census Bureau 1997, table A). As a result, the majority of female beneficiaries still draw benefits on the basis of their husbands' earnings, as spouses or widows. A spouse is entitled to a payment equal to 50 percent of her spouse's benefit or a benefit based on her own earnings, whichever is higher. As a widow, she is entitled to the benefit formerly received by her husband. A woman whose benefit was based on her husband's earnings will find that her household income drops from 150 percent of her husband's benefits to 100 percent when she is widowed, leaving her with two-thirds of her prior household income when it generally takes about 80 percent to maintain the same standard of living. The situation is even worse for a married woman whose benefits are based on her own work record. For example, if both spouses had the same benefit, she will end up with half her prior household income upon the death of her husband.

These and other inequities, including the unconscionably high poverty rates among elderly women living alone, should be the targets of real Social Security reform. But no influential voices are calling for this kind of change. Instead we are bombarded with proposals for cuts—regressive, unnecessary, and impoverishing cuts—and various privatization schemes.

In an atmosphere so clouded by misinformation and disinformation, it would be risky for those who wish to preserve Social Security to jump on the "reform" bandwagon in the hope of actually improving the system. In fact, it is difficult to think of a worse time in the last six decades to open up Social Security to any kind of legislative changes. Real reform will have to wait until rational discussion can take place—and so will any measures to augment the program's revenues, should these prove necessary.

Fortunately, there is no financial or economic imperative to do anything soon. In fact the latest projections of the system's actuaries just added another two years to the reformers' dreaded day of reckoning—now 2034—compared to the previous year's projections. (And, as noted in chapter 4, changes in the consumer price index that have yet to be incorporated would add another 4–11 years.) So if they thought that now was the time to act, they now have two more years to ruminate.

A 10- to 15-year hiatus from this debate might be just what the country needs. Perhaps by then the political climate will have changed, and attacking programs for the elderly will once again be seen as cowardly rather than as a sign of political courage.

7 | The Debate over National Saving

THE CONVENTIONAL WISDOM SAYS that the nation's big problem is that it is not saving enough for the future. If the nation as a whole would just save more money each year, then there would be more investment, the economy would grow more rapidly, and we all would be rich in the near future. If we take this road, the advice goes, it will be no problem to pay for the retirement or health care expenses of the baby boom generation.

The effort to increase growth by increasing saving is important to the Social Security debate because, unless the economy's growth rate increases, the only way to give more to future generations of workers will be to take it from future retirees. Most advocates of privatizing Social Security claim that they actually want to increase the income of future retirees compared with the benefits promised by Social Security. But unless their plans actually increase the economy's growth rate, higher incomes for future retirees will mean lower living standards for the working population.

The drive to increase saving takes place in policy discussions of both public and private saving. As for public saving, the drive to eliminate the budget deficit has been a central goal of public policy for the last 15 years. A federal budget deficit means the national government is borrowing, subtracting from total national savings. Now that the budget appears to have a small surplus, the federal government is finally adding to national savings rather than subtracting from it.

At the private level, Americans are known to be poor savers. Most studies show that Americans save a much smaller percentage of their incomes each year than do people in almost every other industrialized nation. As a result, our national savings rate ranks near the bottom. The policy prescriptions to address the problem center on creating incentives to save by changing tax policy—incorporating lower marginal income tax rates, eliminating or reducing the capital gains tax, or replacing the income tax with a sales tax.

While stronger growth and a more prosperous future sound good, increased saving is not necessarily the way to get us there. The argument for the connection between higher saving and higher growth turns out to be considerably more complicated than generally recognized. The connection is at best indirect, if present at all. Furthermore, the impact on growth of any likely increase in the savings rate will be far less than is generally recognized. Even the most optimistic savings scenarios presents us with a world in 2030 that differs little from the one in current, low-savings projections. In other words, if there's a big demographic problem, it won't go away by saving.

In the sections that follow we examine the debate on saving in more detail. The first section discusses the meaning of saving in an economic context and explains how higher saving can be linked to higher levels of investment. The second section explains the process through which higher saving can lead to higher investment. The third section explains why it is so difficult to raise savings rates through government policy. The fourth section examines the potential impact of higher rates of investment on economic growth and the future size of the economy.

An Economist's View of Saving

The words "investment" and "saving" tend to mean different things to economists and noneconomists. Behavior that people generally refer to as "investment" doesn't make the grade in the economist's definition. And many actions that seem far removed from saving to most people will fit the economist's definition. Since the definitions are closely tied to the way economists perceive the economy as operating, it is worth spending a bit of time on the semantics.

To an economist, "investment" means the purchase of a newly produced physical asset, such as a factory, a truck, or a computer, that will increase the economy's productive capacity in the future. The connection of investment with a new physical asset is important, because individuals often think of themselves as investing when there is no new physical asset being created. For example, a person may buy a share of stock, a government bond, or a parcel of real estate as an investment. In this case, he or she hopes to have more money in the future as a result of buying one of these assets. But from the standpoint of the economy as a whole, this purchase is not an investment. The purchase of one of these assets simply redistributes existing assets—it does not increase the ability of the economy to produce goods or services in the future.

Similarly, many corporate "investments" would not fall within the economist's definition. A corporation may buy a factory or a line of software from one of its competitors, or it may buy one of its competitors outright in a merger. The corporation would view these actions as investments that will lead to increased profits. An economist would disagree since, by themselves, none of these actions increase the economy's ability to produce goods and services in the future; they simply redistribute ownership of existing assets. Like the earlier set of actions, they just involve shifting pieces of paper: a deed to a factory, ownership of a patent or a trademark, or stock certificates. To an economist, investment means creating new physical assets, not just shuffling around ones that already exist. It is only the creation of new physical assets—computers, machinery, factories—that will actually increase the economy's productive capacities in the future. This point must constantly be kept in mind if one is to understand the issues in the debate over saving and investment.

As to saving, most people probably think of it as a deliberate act. A person might be thought to save when he or she deposits money in a savings account, purchases a government bond, or buys a share of stock. For most people, saving means the decision to put money aside for the future. Economists take a somewhat different view: saving means simply not spending, and that can include not only all the things that people generally view as saving but also other acts as well. For example, if I plan to purchase a car this week but have not yet gotten around to it, then I have saved in the economist's lexicon. If I keep my money under my mattress, I have saved in an economic sense. In fact, if I destroy my money by burning it in an act of protest, I have saved in an economic sense. As long as I have not spent my money on an item of current consumption, an economist would view me as saving.

The distinction between the economists' view of saving and the more colloquial definition is important because it calls attention to the way in which economists view saving as increasing investment and economic growth. This view is quite different from what most people believe.

Furthermore, with regard to saving, it is common to believe that my decision to save will lead to more investment, because I will lend my money, either directly or indirectly, to a company that wants to borrow it to finance

Chapter Seven

investment. I can make such a loan directly by buying shares of stock, or I can make the loan indirectly by lending money to a bank, which will in turn lend it to a business. In this way, there is a fairly simple and direct link between the decision to save and the decision to invest.

The government can also get pulled into the picture in the sense that it is another borrower in the financial arena. If the government borrows a dollar to finance its deficit, there is one less dollar available for private investment. In this way, when the deficit declines, money is freed up for investment.

The purchase of stock provides a good example of the disjunction between a consumer's view of investment and an economist's. There is nothing about an individual's purchase of a share of stock that requires anyone to increase his or her investment. In all probability, the stock purchased is a share the company issued long ago, and the money will go not to the company to finance investment, but rather to another shareholder who has decided to sell his or her stock. This shareholder might use the money to buy a car or take a vacation; there is no reason to believe that the seller will use it to undertake any sort of investment.

The decision to buy the share of stock does, though, increase demand for the stock and, in that way, lifts its price. A higher share price means that a company can raise more capital by selling shares, since it can get more money for each share it sells. In this way, the decision to buy a share of stock may make it cheaper for the corporation to invest. But higher share prices do not typically have any direct impact on investment, since companies finance a very small part of their investment by selling stock. In fact, even with the huge run-up in stock prices in the last 15 years, companies are actually buying more stock than they are selling.[1] This means that corporations are actually net lenders to the stock market, not borrowers from it.

Similarly, if we lend our money to a bank by putting it in a savings account, we have in no way guaranteed that the bank will lend the money to finance some type of investment; rather, the bank will lend the money to whichever borrower appears to be the best customer, which could be a business that wants to expand, credit card holders, or a corporation that wants to finance a corporate takeover.

1. According to data from the Federal Reserve Board, on net corporations purchased $79.2 billion more in stock than they issued in 1997 (Flow of Fund Accounts, March 1998, table F213).

In short, our decision to save does not lead directly to an increase in investment. It may make more money available to be borrowed, but there is nothing that we can do to ensure that this money will actually be borrowed to finance new investment; it can, and probably will, be borrowed for some altogether different purpose. Furthermore, there are other ways to make additional funds available for borrowing that do not require any act of saving whatsoever. This means that, insofar as an increased supply of funds available to be borrowed actually can increase investment, additional saving is neither necessary nor sufficient to bring about this result.

While saving in the colloquial sense may not directly lead to investment, most economists would argue that there is a link between saving, in the sense of not spending, and investment. The argument is that, by not spending money on some type of current consumption (whatever goods or services might otherwise have been consumed) resources have been freed up for investment. In other words, because I did not spend my money on a car, a restaurant meal, or a new suit, the resources (labor, material, and physical capital) that would have otherwise been used to produce these items are now free to make investment goods. In this view, the only fact that is important is that I did not spend my money on consumption. If I bought a government bond or a share of stock, deposited my money in a savings account, put off buying a car, stuffed my money under my mattress, or burned it, from the perspective of those who advocate higher growth through higher saving, all of these actions are equally good.

How Saving Generates Investment

If saving simply means not spending on current consumption, and thereby freeing up resources (labor, raw materials, or physical capital) for investment, what is the mechanism which ensures that these resources are used for investment? If I and all my friends stop going to our favorite restaurants, we might think that the impact of our behavior is that these restaurants go out of business and their workers lose their jobs, not that investment increases. However, in the economist's view, the fact that these workers lost their jobs would place downward pressure on wages, and the fact that there are vacant storefronts might place downward pressure on rents or real estate prices. The fall in wages and rents (and possibly in other factors as well) will make some investment possibilities appear more profitable. If these prices fall far enough, eventually the unemployed workers will be hired for other jobs and the vacant storefronts will be reopened for other purposes. If my restaurant spending is not replaced by some other type of consumption spending, then this other purpose will be investment.

This process can be hastened along by the actions of the nation's monetary authority, the Federal Reserve Board. The role of the Federal Reserve Board in this story is to take note of the fact that large numbers of people have curtailed their restaurant dining, creating slack in the form of unemployed workers and other idle resources. The Fed can, in effect, print money, thereby increasing the amount of funds available to the banking system to lend. This step will cause interest rates to fall. In this way, the Fed can give firms greater incentive to undertake new investment, thereby facilitating the process whereby the unemployed workers and idle resources are reemployed and produce investment goods that will make the nation richer in the future.

Ways to Boost Saving and Investment

In standard economic theory, saving means simply not consuming, and the particular way in which an individual chooses to save does not affect the economy. Therefore, in standard economic theory, all of the following are equally effective ways to use savings to support investment:

- placing $1 million in a checking account
- placing $1 million in a savings account
- placing $1 million in the stock market
- buying $1 million in government bonds
- placing $1 million under a mattress
- burning $1 million

Since saving simply means not spending, thereby freeing resources for investment, any decision that frees resources will be equally effective in promoting investment. Thus, all of the following decisions will be equally effective in stimulating investment, according to standard economic theory:

- the cancellation of $1 million in government contracts for new planes
- a reduction in the government payroll of $1 million
- the cancellation of $1 million in foreign orders for U.S. planes
- a reduction of $1 million in consumer spending on air travel
- a reduction of $1 million in consumer spending on new cars

Through its control of the nation's money supply, the Federal Reserve Board can increase the supply of funds available for borrowing in a way that is completely independent of the decision of individuals to save. The Federal Reserve Board can put more money into the banking system any time that it considers appropriate. It is also possible for the banking system itself, through financial innovations, to increase the supply of funds available for lending. For example, in the late 1970s, banks began to offer money market accounts that allowed individuals to earn interest on money that would have otherwise been in non-interest-paying checking accounts. Under existing regulations, banks were able to lend out a larger portion of the money from these money market accounts than from traditional checking accounts, and thus banks could lend out more money even though there was no new money in the banking system. Over the years, creative financiers have developed dozens of such innovations, the impact of which is to remove any direct relationship between the decision of people to save and the amount of money available to be lent out.

To sum up, the path from greater saving to greater investment first involves a contraction of demand. This leads firms to lay off workers and to inactivate other resources, which in turn causes wages and the prices of other inputs to fall. At the same time the Federal Reserve Board can cause interest rates to fall. Together, these actions will provide incentives for firms to reemploy the laid-off workers and utilize the idle resources for producing investment goods.

There are many important and empirically questionable assumptions in this logical chain. First, it is crucial that the fall in wages, real estate prices, and other input prices or interest rates do not simply provide a stimulus to some other type of consumption spending. For example, the decision by my friends and me to stop going to restaurants may have led to lower prices for haircuts, and now everyone is getting haircuts more frequently. In this case our decision to increase our savings did not increase investment at all. It simply led others to consume more.

Second, it is important to recognize that the driving force for increasing investment in this story is a fall in demand, not a decision to save for the future. It is the fall in demand that frees up resources and creates downward pressure on wages, other input prices, and interest rates, not my decision to save. In this sense, any fall in demand is equally good. This means, for example, that the decision by a foreign airline to cancel a $5 billion airplane order from Boeing provides exactly the same stimulus to investment as a $5 billion reduction in the federal budget deficit or the decision by households to save an additional $5 billion. Similarly, a decision to cancel other investments, for example, a decision by General Motors to cancel plans for a $2 billion car factory, provides just as much stimulus to new investment as the decision to increase saving by $2 billion. In both these cases resources are freed up in precisely the same manner as when people choose to save more or when the government reduces the budget deficit. Therefore, they have exactly the same stimulatory effect on investment. From the standpoint of this view—that increased saving is the way to promote investment—lowered exports or canceled investment plans will provide just as much stimulus to new investment as increased private saving or a lower budget deficit.

The third and most important assumption in this story is that the economy is already at full employment, meaning that every worker who is willing to work at the prevailing wage already has a job; and that the economy's productive capacity—its factories, mines, stores, and commercial real estate—is being fully utilized.[2] This assumption is crucial, because if there are already unemployed workers or idle resources, adding to the unemployment rolls or further decreasing demand in factories by reducing consumption is not likely to provide any incentive to invest; the labor and other resources that firms need to undertake additional investment are already available. The firms just need to be convinced that such investment will be profitable.

The view that investment is not generally limited by saving because the economy is not generally at full employment dominated the economics profession from the end of the Great Depression until the mid-1970s. Most often associated with British economist John Maynard Keynes, this view held that the economy has a tendency to operate at below its full-employment level

---

2. This does not have to be taken to mean literally that there is no unemployment or that all factories are running at 100 percent of capacity. Some workers will always be between jobs, and some workers will choose not to work given the wage that their skills would command. Even when the economy is fully employed, some of these people will be counted as unemployed. Exactly what unemployment rate would correspond to full employment is a topic of considerable debate among economists. Similarly, full capacity in industry does not mean that all firms are operating at 100 percent capacity. Most firms typically operate with some amount of excess capacity, thus allowing equipment to be maintained and leaving firms ready to meet any unexpected surges in demand. The level of capacity utilization that corresponds to full capacity cannot be precisely determined, but it is somewhat less than 100 percent.

of output. According to Keynes, the chain of causation generally went from investment to saving. When firms opted to undertake more investment, demand in the economy was increased, leading to higher employment and output as firms increased production to meet this new demand. Higher employment and output would lead to more saving in the economy, since workers who had been unemployed would now have jobs and income from which they could save. Similarly, the government would be saving more, since higher output means more tax revenue and therefore a lower budget deficit or a higher surplus.

Keynes believed that it would generally be futile to try to increase investment by increasing saving. If the economy was below full employment, then the decision of people to save more (i.e., to consume less) meant that they would buy fewer goods and services from businesses. If businesses saw a reduction in their demand, their natural response would be to cut back production and lay off workers, not increase investment. In fact, if firms see less current demand for their products, they may actually opt to decrease investment, since they may believe that they already have enough plant and equipment to meet the demand levels they are likely to see in the future. In this scenario, the decision by individuals or the government to increase saving may actually lead to lower investment, as has happened recently in Japan.

The Keynesian view of the economy probably corresponds to the way in which most people view it as operating. In public discussions, most people do not generally speak as though they consider the economy to be at full employment, and an argument that a particular policy would create a large number of new jobs is seen as an important consideration. Also, most people would view a decision by a foreign airline to cancel plane orders from Boeing as bad news for the U.S. economy, not as a chance for increased investment.

The only way that a policy can create jobs in an economy that is already fully employed is by increasing its overall efficiency, thus persuading some workers who were not willing to work at the wage their skills previously commanded to enter the labor force to earn the new, higher wage. Since the impact of almost any policy on the economy's overall level of efficiency is extremely small, the impact on the labor market would also be small. For example, a worker may opt to sit home watching television when the best wage he could command is $7.00 per hour. A policy that increases the economy's overall efficiency by 0.5 percent (an extremely large improvement compared to most policies subject to public debate) would raise this person's wage by 3.5 cents

Chapter Seven

Creating Jobs in a Full-Employment Economy

In standard economic theory, most unemployment is essentially voluntary: the people counted as unemployed actually could work at the wage their skills command but opt instead for leisure. By this view, when a policy leads to more jobs, it is because it increases the economy's efficiency, thereby pushing up the wages of all workers, including the wages available to previously unemployed workers. However, these wage gains are likely to be small.

For example, some economists estimated that the 1994 General Agreement on Tariffs and Trade (GATT) might increase the economy's efficiency by approximately 0.5 percentage points, thereby creating approximately 400,000 additional jobs. Although 400,000 new jobs might seem a big gain, according to the standard theory the new workers are people who decided that a 0.5 percentage point increase in the available wage made it worthwhile to work rather than stay at home. The gain in the mind of these 400,000 new workers is thus no larger than the typical wage gain in the economy. In the case of a worker receiving $8.00 an hour, the average gain would be a 4-cent-an-hour pay increase; for a worker receiving $20 an hour, it would be approximately a 10-cent-an-hour wage increase. In standard economic theory, the gain to those switching from unemployment to employment is no larger than these modest wage gains.

per hour. At this wage, the person may decide to work instead of sit at home. Only unemployed people who could be persuaded to work by such modest wage increases would be added to the labor force in this way.

It is important to note that the switch from unemployment to employment is of little gain even to these people. These workers could have found employment at a slightly lower wage, but they opted not to work. Now that the wage is slightly higher, they find they are somewhat better off working than not working. A policy that ostensibly provides gains in efficiency may make these newly employed workers marginally better off, but the shift from unemployment to employment is not a qualitative jump in well-being in this scenario, where unemployment is the result of a voluntary decision not to work at the prevailing wage.

In political debate, unemployment is generally viewed as a real hardship, not a voluntary decision by workers hoping for a slightly higher wage. However, for reasons that have never been fully explained, the Keynesian view fell out of favor in the economics profession in the 1970s.[3] Since then a pre-Keynesian view, that saving determines investment, has again taken hold. This is not the place to determine the relative merits of the two views; the purpose of this discussion is simply to point out the logic of the view that saving causes investment. Those who choose to accept this view of the economy must also accept the logical implications of this position.

Finding a Recipe for Higher Saving

If we believe that the way to increase investment is to increase saving, then we need to figure out how to increase saving. Some simple answers to this question turn out to be not very good. One is to increase private saving by increasing incentives for individuals to save. Such incentives can include lower overall tax rates, special tax breaks for saving, or lower capital gains rates. A second answer is to increase public saving by reducing the government's budget deficit or increasing the surplus. Since national saving is the sum of public and private saving, we can increase national saving by increasing public saving while holding private saving constant.

Increasing private saving through tax incentives is not easy. President Reagan tried it in his "supply-side" tax cuts in 1981. By reducing income tax rates, particularly for the wealthy, people were supposed to have more incentive to save. In fact, saving appeared to decline across the income spectrum (see Bosworth, Burtless, and Sabelhaus 1991). More targeted proposals, such as expanded individual retirement accounts or 401(k) defined-contribution pension plans, have a slightly better record: there is some evidence that they have led to higher saving,[4] although the ambiguity in the evidence suggests that the effect, if there is one, is probably not very large. Also, it is important to remember that any plan to increase private saving through tax incentives must generate enough private saving to compensate for the lost government revenue before it leads, on net, to an increase in national saving.

---

3. Part of the explanation for the collapse of the neo-Keynesian view was its failure to provide a full explanation of the stagflation of the late 1970s. Keynesian theory could easily explain high inflation and low unemployment, or low inflation and high unemployment, but high inflation occurring at a time of relatively high unemployment required a somewhat more complex explanation.

4. Poterba, Venti, and Wise (1996) find evidence that 401(k) plans have led to higher levels of saving. Engen, Gale, and Scholz (1996) find that 401(k) plans have primarily reallocated saving between different types of assets rather than led to a significant net increase in savings.

Chapter Seven

The problem that any plan to increase private saving through incentives encounters is that there are always two effects from any tax incentive. On the one hand, the incentive provides a greater return for saving. For example, if I can accumulate interest tax free, then my after-tax return is going to be higher; this should encourage me to save more. On the other hand, any saving incentive will also mean that people can accumulate the same amount of wealth by saving less. If people save for some specific purpose, such as their children's education or to support their own retirement, savings incentives will allow them to reach their goal by putting less aside each year than would have been necessary in the absence of these incentives. In practice, these two effects are partially offsetting, meaning that any increase in private saving due to government incentives is likely to be limited.[5]

A better way to increase saving is through rapid income growth. The basic story here is quite simple. People develop a certain standard of living that they attempt to maintain through time. If their income falls, they will attempt to maintain the same standard of living by reducing their saving, and then by borrowing. If this eventually becomes impossible, then households will adopt a lower standard of living they can support with a lower level of income. In contrast, if income rises rapidly, people will not immediately adjust their standard of living upward by the same amount. Their initial response will be to save much of the increase in income and only gradually adjust their living standard upward.

This simple story seems to fit the evidence quite well. Carroll and Summers (1990) found a strong link between rising incomes and higher savings rates. If this view is correct, then the best way to increase private savings is through broadly based income gains. Achieving such gains may not be easy—most families have seen stagnant or declining incomes in the last two decades as income has shifted upward—but significantly increasing private savings rates may be impossible otherwise.[6]

---

5. One possible side effect of a shift to a privatized Social Security system is a reduction in other private saving, a likely outcome if people view the money placed in a government-mandated savings account as a substitute for money they currently save in individual retirement accounts or 401(k) plans. If this happened, privatizing Social Security might actually lead to lower national saving.

6. Opponents of Social Security, most prominently Martin Feldstein, Harvard professor and former chairman of the Council of Economic Advisors, assert that Social Security has been a major factor in lowering private saving. In a 1974 study Feldstein reported evidence

If we cannot with certainty raise private saving through tax incentives, can we raise public saving by lowering the budget deficit or increasing the surplus? We in fact just had an opportunity to test this plan, and it didn't work either. In 1989, the peak of the last business cycle, the budget deficit was $152.5 billion, or approximately 2.8 percent of gross domestic product (GDP).[7] By 1997, the budget deficit had dropped to $21.9 billion, or 0.3 percent of GDP. This 2.5 percentage point drop in the deficit as a share of GDP constituted a very large increase in public saving. Given this increase in national saving, the sum of domestic investment and foreign investment should have risen by 2.5 percentage points of GDP.[8] But the gain was far smaller, just 0.3 percentage points of GDP,[9] because the increase in public saving was offset

---

of a negative relationship between Social Security wealth and private saving. His finding turned out to be the result of a computer error; when it was corrected, the result was no longer statistically significant. Feldstein repeated this study using more data in 1995 (Feldstein 1995) and reported again that he found that Social Security wealth reduced private saving. However, he has refused requests to make his data available so that an outside researcher can verify his findings.

7. Using a business cycle peak minimizes the effect of cyclical changes on the deficit and the economy. It is standard for economists to compare the economy at business cycle peaks in order to distinguish between the impact of the business cycle and underlying features of the economy. It is also standard to measure the deficit relative to the size of the economy in order to get a clear idea of its magnitude. A $200 billion deficit is not very large in an $8,500 billion economy, roughly the size of the economy in 1998, but it would have been quite large in 1960, when the nation's GDP was $527 billion.

8. In national income accounting, national saving (the sum of private and public saving) is equal to the sum of domestic and net foreign investment. Like domestic investment, net foreign investment increases the nation's future wealth. If the United States has increased its net holdings of foreign financial assets (e.g., shares of stock or bonds of foreign corporations, bonds issued by foreign governments, factories or real estate in foreign countries), then it will be able to get more dividends, interest, or profits from these assets in the future. These payments will in turn allow the United States to consume more imports from other nations than it would otherwise.

It is important to remember that it is *net* foreign assets that matter. Just as foreign assets held by the United States make us richer by allowing us to import more in the future than we would otherwise, domestic assets held by foreigners make us poorer by requiring that we export more, thus leaving fewer goods and services to be consumed domestically. Only if our net holdings of foreign assets increase (i.e., we buy more foreign assets than foreigners buy U.S. assets) is the nation made better off.

9. Measured as a share of GDP, investment in the four quarters of fiscal year 1997 was 12.4 percent, exactly the same as in 1989. Both years saw a trade deficit, which implies

Chapter Seven

by a reduction in private saving (consumption rose as a share of GDP by 1.8 percentage points). Thus, the effort to increase national saving failed.

Perhaps this outcome should not be surprising. The causal link from lower budget deficits to higher investment is supposed, primarily, to be lower real interest rates. However, the real interest rate did not fall as a result of the deficit reduction plans put in place in the 1990s. In fact, from 1993 to 1997 it was slightly higher than what the Congressional Budget Office (CBO) had projected at the beginning of 1993, before the Clinton deficit reduction package was even proposed.[10]

Although it is central to the view that saving causes investment, the evidence that lower deficits lead to lower interest rates is limited. Economists have studied the topic for years, but the evidence has been mixed: some studies have found a link between lower deficits and lower interest rates, but many others have found little or no relationship.[11] At best, the relationship between lower deficits and lower interest rates can be viewed as one that has some theoretical basis but limited empirical support.

The case for the second linkage—between lower interest rates and increased investment—is far weaker. Studies have generally found that lower

negative net foreign investment, but it was slightly less negative in 1997, 1.2 percent of GDP compared with 1.5 percent of GDP in 1989.

10. The average real interest rate on 10-year government bonds projected for these years in January 1993 was 3.8 percent (CBO 1993, xv). The actual real interest rate was 3.9 percent.

11. For two surveys that discuss many of these studies, see Thomas and Abderrezak 1988 and Barth et al. 1991. One reason it is hard to get good answers about the relationship between interest rates and the government deficit is that it is difficult to fully account for cyclical effects and the impact of expectations. The cyclical impact is important because we know that the deficit will rise every time the economy moves into a downturn. However, an increase in the deficit due to a recession is expected to be associated with lower real interest rates. On the other hand, a higher deficit at a business cycle peak should in principle lead to higher interest rates. It is necessary, but not easy, to accurately control for the cyclical movement in the deficit in order to focus on the effect of changes in the deficit that are structural (i.e., independent of the business cycle). The role of expectations is important because the issue under examination is long-term interest rates. Thus, it is not just the current deficit that should matter but also expectations about future deficits. If the current deficit is high but a credible plan for deficit reduction is in place, then interest rates should fall in anticipation of the lower deficits expected in the future. Since we can't know with certainty what people expect to happen in the future, it is not easy to say how real interest rates will respond to the expectation of future deficits.

real interest rates lead to higher levels of investment, but the impact is very small.[12]

Interest rates are one of the factors that influence investment, but not a very important one. In an extensive analysis that examined the investment behavior of more than 5,000 firms over a 20-year period, Washington University professor Steve Fazzari (1993) found that interest rates were far less important than were firms' cash flow and sales growth in determining the level of investment. For the smaller, faster-growing firms in this sample, the real interest rate had no impact at all: *only* sales growth and cash flow mattered. This finding should probably not be very surprising. Firms invest when they are flush with cash from high profits and when they see rapid growth in sales. Lower interest rates may reduce the cost of borrowing, but if the demand for a firm's products is not strong, lower interest rates by themselves are not going to support investment. The results imply that lowering interest rates is a poor way to stimulate investment. The results are also consistent with the scenario that it was consumption, not investment, that increased as a result of the last round of deficit reduction.

The Impact of Investment on Economic Growth

The assumption behind the arguments for deficit reduction or saving incentive plans is that, if national saving were sufficiently high, the economy would grow to the point where the retirement of the baby boom generation would not be a burden. But even if we can find a way to increase national saving, we still don't know how much this will increase economic growth.

Unfortunately, the evidence linking higher saving to faster growth is fairly skimpy. The CBO contrasted a scenario in which the government ran a balanced budget every year from 1996 to 2030 with a scenario in which it ran annual deficits of $200 billion (an amount that would maintain a constant debt-to-GDP ratio). In both scenarios the economy was projected to be substantially larger in 2030 than it is at present. The difference in growth between the two paths was relatively modest. In 2030, the additional saving in the balanced-budget path raised national income by 1.6 percent compared to the deficit path (see fig. 7-1). But with the economy in 2030 projected to be growing by 1.3 percent a year, it will take the country just 15 months to make

---

12. See Chirinko 1993 for a survey of the evidence on the link between interest rates and investment.

Chapter Seven

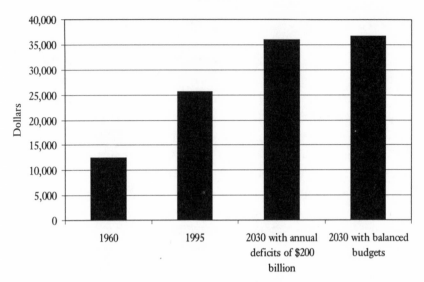

Figure 7-1. Saving Our Way to a Better Future? Real Per Capita Income Under Balanced Budget and Annual Deficit Scenarios

up the lost ground. This means that the difference between running $200-billion-plus deficits every year and keeping the budget in balance is that, in the balanced-budget scenario, we will be as rich on January 1, 2030, as we would be on April 1, 2031 under the high-deficit scenario. If the proponents of higher national saving thought that we would be poor in the future if we continued on a path of running deficits, they'll find no support in this CBO study.

Even more optimistic assumptions about the potential for increasing saving would not change this picture. Suppose we could increase national saving by *twice* as much as the movement to a balanced budget we just discussed. As a simple approximation, we can assume that the income gains would be double what the CBO projected in the earlier comparison,[13] or 3.2 percent higher in 2030 than in the low-saving path. To compare points in time, the high-saving route will make us as rich on January 1, 2030, as we would otherwise be on July 1, 2032, 30 months later. This sort of increase in income might be desir-

13. In reality the gains should be less than twice as large. Most of the income gain from higher saving will be the result of an increase in the size of the capital stock. There are diminishing returns to capital (as with any factor of production), so that the effect of doubling the increase in the capital stock should be less than twice as large as the increase in national income calculated by the CBO.

able, but it is not going to qualitatively change the situation for our children and grandchildren. If they are going to be burdened on the low-saving path, then they will also be burdened on the high-saving path.

One of the ironies of many proposals for Social Security privatization is that they promise better returns for future retirees without offering much prospect of increasing overall economic growth. But if retirees in the year 2030 actually have more income under a privatization scheme than under the current Social Security system, and if the economy were no larger than it would be with the existing Social Security system, then these proposals will actually place *more* of a burden on our children and grandchildren. In other words, if a privatization plan has not increased the size of the pie in 2030, but the plan allows retirees to get more pie, then there must be less left for everyone else. In this case, a proposal advanced as a way to reduce the burden placed on future generations will actually increase it.

Saving Will Not Make Us Rich

The link from higher saving to higher investment is quite tenuous. Investment can lead directly to higher saving by increasing income, but the link in the opposite direction, from higher saving to higher investment, is indirect. Moreover, it is difficult to design policies that will actually lead to higher levels of national saving, and even if we could, the effect of saving on economic growth has been greatly exaggerated.

In principle it is possible that the economy can enjoy significantly more rapid growth, which would make people qualitatively better off. In the years from the end of World War II until 1973, productivity in the economy increased by 2.5 percent a year. Since 1973, it has increased by just 1.1 percent a year, and most projections expect this slow-growth path to continue. It is not clear why productivity growth has slowed. Less investment was a factor, but a relatively unimportant one. Higher rates of saving and investment in the future could push this growth rate up by 0.1 or 0.2 percentage points, but while this is desirable, this boost does not come close to getting us back to the growth rates of the early postwar years. If we can regain the productivity growth rates of the 1950s and 1960s, our children and grandchildren will be much better off. But higher savings will not restore the golden age.

8 | Will the Age Wave Lift All Boats?

ANY OF THE CRITICS of Social Security have painted an image of a dismal future in which aging baby boomers place a crushing burden on the generations that follow them. Former Secretary of the United States Commerce Department Peter Peterson looks at the demographic trends and warns that the United States will become a "nation of Floridas," where retirement homes and golf courses dominate the landscape and where the elderly live the good life at the expense of their children and grandchildren.

In 1995 the cover of the *New York Times Magazine* featured an image that posed the issue somewhat more seriously and far more poignantly. It showed a young couple walking in a park. The man pushed the wheelchair of an elderly person, presumably a parent, and the woman pushed a stroller while a second young child walked closely behind. The question posed by the picture and the article was how a future generation of young people could care for both their aging parents and their young children.

It is easy to draw negative images about a future in which the population will be considerably older than it is now. Under any scenario, there will be far more retirees relative to the size of the working population in 2030 than there are today. But will that demographic trend necessarily dominate our lives? Indeed, what will life look like 20 or 30 years from now, when most of the baby boom generation will have reached retirement age? By carrying current trends forward and reflecting on the likely course of future developments, we should be able to derive some general sense of what the country will look like in the first decades of the next century.

Will the Age Wave Lift All Boats?

The Basic Features of the Future

The projections discussed in chapter 2 showed that, on average, people should be far better off in 2020 or 2030 than they are today, even if they have to pay a somewhat larger share of their income in taxes to support Social Security, Medicare, and other programs that benefit the elderly. In a scenario in which taxes increase as needed to support the aging of the population, the typical family will have a 13.9 percent higher after-tax income (after adjusting for inflation) in 2010 than it did in 1995. By 2030, its after-tax income will be more than 30 percent higher. And these projections of solid (though perhaps not exciting) income growth are based on relatively pessimistic projections about productivity growth in the report of the Social Security trustees. They assume that productivity will grow through this period at approximately a 1.3 percent annual rate, only slightly higher than the 1.1 percent rate of the last 25 years and well below the 2.5 percent rate of the period from 1947 to 1973.[1] The projections therefore assume that the economy is never able to rebound to the more rapid pace of productivity growth that the United States experienced through most of its history. Moreover, the projections imply that the United States is unable to achieve the same productivity growth rates as Western European countries with comparable living standards. Many of these countries, such as France, Belgium, and Denmark, have managed to maintain productivity growth rates of approximately 2.0 percent annually. Since wage growth on average tracks productivity growth, these nations are in a position

---

1. The rate of income growth in these projections also does not factor in the effect of recent changes in the consumer price index (CPI), which should lead to some increase in the rate of real income growth. Real income growth is defined as nominal income growth minus the rate of inflation. The Bureau of Labor Statistics (BLS) has made changes in the way it computes the CPI since 1995, and these changes will cause it to record a lower rate of inflation in the future than in the past. The Council of Economic Advisors estimates that these changes will reduce the measured rate of inflation by 0.69 percentage points annually (*ERP* 1998, 80). If its assessment of the impact of these changes is correct, then if the old CPI would have shown a rate of inflation of 2.69 percent, the new CPI would show a rate of 2.0 percent. Thus, if real wage growth had been projected to be 0.9 percent annually when measured against the old CPI, it should be 1.59 percent annually (0.9 percent plus 0.69 percent) when measured against the new CPI. The recent changes in the CPI will probably not lower the measured rate of inflation by a full 0.69 percent indefinitely, but they nevertheless will lead to a somewhat lower measured rate of inflation, meaning that the rate of projected real wage growth should be somewhat more rapid than under the old CPI.

to soar past the United States in prosperity in the first decades of the next century.

Projections for future income would be even rosier if we were to accept the conclusion of the Boskin Commission (which, as discussed in chapter 4, we probably should not) that the CPI is currently overstated by approximately 1.1 percent annually.[2] If this is the case, then real wages and income are growing by 1.1 percentage points more each year than current data show, and therefore families will be far wealthier in the next century than at present. The after-tax income of a typical family will be nearly 34 percent higher in 2010 than in 1995, and will be 90 percent higher in 2030.

Our projection for the future also assumes that couples will have fewer children. While this trend means fewer future workers to pay Social Security taxes, it also means fewer children to look after and thus lower expenditures on child care, children's doctor bills, clothes, and the other expenses and time associated with raising children. According to the projections in the trustees' report, there will be 0.42 children under age 20 for every adult aged 20–65 in 2020, down from 0.5 in 1995. This trend should leave workers of this period with considerably more income to spend on other things.

Anticipated unemployment rates also affect the trustees' projections. The trustees selected an unemployment rate of 6.0 percent throughout the first 75 years of the next century, derived from recent estimates of the lowest unemployment rate that the economy can sustain without experiencing accelerating inflation (see, e.g., CBO 1994; Weiner 1993; and Gordon 1990b). This calculation seems hopelessly out of date, now that the economy has been through several years in which the unemployment rate has been below 6.0 percent and the inflation rate has decelerated. Moreover, under the labor market situation the trustees project for this period—that of an extreme labor shortage—it might be expected that the unemployment rate will typically be far below 6.0 percent. The trustees project that the labor force will grow by just 2.9 percent from 2010 to 2020 and by just 0.9 percent from 2020 to 2030. By comparison, the labor force grew by 29.2 percent in the 1970s and by 17.7 percent in the 1980s; it grew by 3.1 percent in 1972 alone, about the same growth projected for the period from 2010 to 2020.

---

2. After the changes the BLS recently put in place, the size of the overstatement claimed by the commission will shrink by approximately 0.25 percent, leaving an overstatement of 0.85 percent.

This sort of labor shortage would be good news for most workers: even the least-skilled workers should have their choice of jobs. And the mass retirement of the baby boomers should also be good news for higher-end workers. The senior executives and managers in corporations, government, and nonprofits will be retiring in droves, leaving enormous opportunities for advancement for the generations that follow them.

It is not easy to project exactly how the economy will function in a period in which labor is in such short supply for such a long time, but if history is any guide, the prospects are good for most workers. In the decade from 1950 to 1960, the labor force grew by just 11.9 percent as a result of the low birth rates of the Depression 20 years earlier. During this 10-year period, the unemployment rate averaged 4.5 percent. At some points it fell below 3.0 percent. Real wages also soared in this period. The average hourly wage rose by 27.2 percent from 1950 to 1960, and average hourly compensation rose even more, by 32.7 percent, as more workers received health and pension benefits. As a result of this increase in wages and an increase in the number of workers per family, median family income rose by 37.6 percent over this 10-year period.

This extremely rapid growth in wages and income will not be possible in the period from 2010 to 2030 if the low rate of productivity growth projected by the trustees proves accurate. However, a labor shortage by itself should act to spur productivity growth, for two reasons. First, as workers choose more desirable, better-paying jobs, the lowest-productivity jobs will go unfilled, and the loss of these low-productivity jobs will cause average productivity to rise. Second, businesses have more incentive to find ways to use their workers more productively when they cannot find additional workers easily. This pressure should lead to better organization of workplaces and the use of more laborsaving equipment. Countervailing factors can make it less likely that the second and third decades of the next century will see rapid productivity growth, but it is at least possible that the projected labor shortage will lead to a sharp upswing in productivity growth in these years and therefore a sharp upswing in wage growth.

Before leaving this discussion of the core numbers, one other projection by the trustees is worth noting. Their report projects that the average number of hours worked will decline by 0.1 percent annually. This amount may seem trivial, but over time it will make a significant difference. For example, by 2020 the average workyear will be 2.5 percent shorter than in 1995. For a full-year worker who works 250 days a year, this decline will mean more than six additional days of paid vacation each year by 2020, and 8.5 additional days by 2030. For the millions of workers today who view themselves as constantly pressed for time, the prospect of an additional six or eight days a year in paid vacation probably sounds like a dream come true.

In short, the basic situation of workers and families predicted for the years 2020–30 seems healthy by current standards, even if the future is no brighter than the relatively pessimistic situation projected by the trustees.

The State of the Nation's Health

Discussions of Social Security projections often follow a perverse tack in which the rapid lengthening of life expectancies is referred to as a "pessimistic scenario." From the standpoint of funding Social Security, longer life expectancies are indeed bad news, but most of us probably view the prospect of living longer, healthier lives as great news. While Social Security reformers have focused considerable attention on the pain future generations will suffer as a result of the tax burden needed to support benefits for the elderly, relatively little attention has been paid to what improved health statistics might mean in the lives of future generations.

Life expectancies have been rising throughout this century and are expected to continue to do so in the next century. In 1920, a person born in that year had a life expectancy of just 54.1 years. A baby boomer born in 1960 had a life expectancy of 69.5 years. A child born in the year 2000 will have a life expectancy of 76.6 years. Much of this improvement is attributable to reductions in infant mortality, which has declined in the United States from 76.7 per thousand in 1920 to 7.7 today; it will undoubtedly decline further by 2030.

It is virtually certain that considerable medical progress in the area of diseases will be made by 2030. AIDS presents a case in which, if a cure is not found, treatment will almost certainly be drastically improved, if for no other reason than that the patents that keep the price of some AIDS drugs artificially high will have expired.

The improvements in health care over time have been enormous. Each generation has been able to benefit from health care technology that is a qualitative leap better than the technology available to the previous generation. This pace of improvement should continue into the next century, and as a result, the generations of workers who will support the retirement of the baby boomers from 2020 to 2040 can expect to live much longer and healthier lives than the baby boomers did.

The Many Homes of the Future

As the nation has grown wealthier through time it has improved its housing situation as an ever-growing portion of the population become homeowners. If the projections in the trustees' report prove accurate, these trends should continue over the next 30–40 years.

At present, roughly 65.4 percent of households own their own homes (Department of Commerce 1997, table 1200). This is the highest rate ever, although it follows 17 years in which the homeownership rate was virtually stagnant. During this period, median family income rose very modestly as income instead flowed upward to the more wealthy. During more typical periods, the homeownership rate has consistently risen. For example, from 1950 to 1970 the homeownership rate rose from 55 to 62 percent, an astounding increase of 0.35 percentage points a year. If income growth proceeds at an even pace in the future, it is not unreasonable to assume that homeownership rates might increase by 0.18 percentage points a year (half the rate of increase from 1950 to 1970), bringing the proportion of households owning their own homes to 69.4 percent in 2020 and to 71.2 percent in 2030.

Not only will a far larger proportion of households own their own homes, but they should also have far better housing. From 1991 to 1996 the nation added 11.9 million units of housing,[3] an average of 2,372,000 per year (Department of Commerce 1997, table 1195). Continuing to add housing at this rate would mean a net increase of 56.9 million units by 2020 and 80.6 million units by 2030,[4] gains of 49.9 percent and 70.7 percent, respectively. Since the nation's population is projected to be 20.2 percent higher in 2020 and 26.1 percent higher in 2030, this means that the ratio of housing units to people will have increased by 24.7 percent in 2020 and by 35.4 percent in

---

3. This is the *net* addition of units, meaning the number of newly constructed units minus the number of units destroyed.

4. It will be possible to increase the number of housing units at the current rate if the same number of workers remain in the construction industry (which would mean that construction declines as a share of total employment), or if increases in productivity offset any absolute decline in the number of workers. Since the number of workers employed in construction has been increasing up to the present, this is probably a very moderate projection. Also, since the number of workers employed constructing offices and factories is certain to decline as the rate of growth of the capital stock slows, more workers will be freed up to build residential housing.

2030. While to some extent there may actually be more units per person, in the form of vacation homes, we can probably view most of the increase as representing an improvement in the quality of housing. Thus, our children and grandchildren should have far nicer housing than we or our parents have.

Benefits of the Information Boom

Information technology is clearly advancing at an extremely rapid rate, and there is no obvious reason to expect the rate to slow. The implications are truly incredible.

For example, according to the BLS, computer prices are now dropping at the rate of 40 percent a year. At this rate, a computer that sells for $2,500 in 1999 will sell for 5 cents in 2020. Either people will spend much less of their income on computers in 2020 or they will be buying much better computers.

By 2020, cellular phone prices should have declined to the point where they are much cheaper than current wired phones. The Internet and Web will have expanded to the point where vast amounts of reading material, recorded music, and films will be instantly available online.[5] Also, the Internet will make it possible to transport this material to virtually anywhere on the planet. The opportunities created by these technologies will dwarf anything our parents could have envisioned during their working lives or even what seemed possible during our own childhood.

Opportunities in Education

There has been a long continuous process in which each generation has attained a level of education exceeding that of the previous generation. This trend may accelerate as smaller cohorts of school-age children translate into lower educational costs.

In 1960, 41 percent of adults over 25 were high school graduates, and fewer than 8.0 percent were college graduates. By 1995, 81.7 percent of adults over 25 were high school graduates, and more than 23 percent had college degrees. If these trends continue at this pace over the next 35 years, by 2030

---

5. The technology will allow this material to be transported virtually without cost, but there may be substantial fees for downloading material from the Web if the nation maintains copyright laws in their current form.

nearly 100 percent of adults will be high school graduates,[6] and more than 40 percent will have college degrees. In addition, the portion of the population receiving postgraduate degrees is also likely to rise significantly. Just 9,800 doctoral degrees were awarded in 1960, compared to 43,200 in 1994 (National Center for Education Statistics 1996, table 168). Assuming that growth is just half as fast in percentage terms over the next 35 years, 95,000 doctorate degrees will be awarded each year by 2030.

Although the tax burden required to support education and other public expenditures on children will fall substantially as the population cohorts decline in size, an important offsetting trend may reduce educational opportunities. The costs of education in general and of college education in particular have risen by considerably more than the overall price level over the last three decades. If this trend continues, then access to college and advanced training may actually become more restricted. It should be an important goal of public policy to ensure that this rate of price increase does not continue.

The Future of Work

A final area worth examining is the workplace. What sorts of jobs will people have in the years 2020 or 2030, and how will they be doing them?

Projecting employment needs for 2030 is difficult, but it is possible to identify some jobs that people will *not* be doing. At the top of the list would be some of the most dangerous and physically demanding jobs that exist today, such as underground mining (although a significant number of workers will no doubt continue to be employed in surface mining of various types). Manufacturing is still likely to be a significant source of employment during these years, although its importance is projected to decline appreciably. According to projections from the BLS (1997), the percentage of the workforce employed in manufacturing will have declined from 15.5 percent in 1996 to 13.3 percent by 2006. If that rate of decline continues, those percentages will fall to 10.2 percent by 2020 and to 8.0 percent by 2030. The nature of these jobs is also likely to change significantly. Factories in 2020 or 2030 will be substantially more automated than they are today, meaning that workers will be far more likely to monitor a process carried through by machines than to engage

---

6. Presumably there will always be some children for whom unusual circumstances prevent the completion of high school.

directly in the production process themselves. This change will require new (but not always greater) skills from workers and less physical exertion.

Employment in health and medical occupations is likely to expand over the next several decades. The portion of the labor force employed in providing medical care increased from 2.9 percent in 1960 to 8.0 percent in 1995,[7] and these numbers are virtually certain to rise in the next century as the demand for medical services increases, in particular among the rapidly growing elderly population. The BLS projects that the demand for doctors will increase by 21.0 percent from 1996 to 2006, the demand for registered nurses by 20.8 percent, and the demand for therapists by 56.3 percent. These trends will continue and probably accelerate in the years after 2010 as the baby boomers reach retirement age. If the growth in these areas simply remains the same as in the recent past, then 0.8 percent of the workforce will be doctors in 2030, 2.7 percent will be nurses, and 1.4 percent will be therapists.

Employment in many other areas will depend on the direction in which technology evolves. Employment has grown rapidly in retail trade over the last 36 years, from 15.2 percent of jobs in 1960 to 17.7 percent in 1996. The BLS projects that retail's share of total employment will remain roughly constant over the next 10 years, although it is easy to imagine a scenario in which retail employment shrinks sharply. For example, if the Internet becomes a major medium for shopping, then the number of people employed in retail stores may decline dramatically in the next few decades.

The financial services sector is also likely to experience significant employment changes. The percentage of the workforce employed in the broad category of financial services, insurance, and real estate increased from 4.8 percent in 1960 to 6.0 percent in 1996, and the BLS projects that the share of employment in this sector will stay at roughly the same level over the next 10 years. Again, it is possible to imagine technology carving a different path. For instance, computerization may radically reduce the need for stockbrokers, insurance dealers, real estate agents, and others employed in providing financial services.

While it may be difficult to identify which areas will be the big gainers in terms of employment, it is clear that the nature of work is likely to change considerably. Most important, computerization should make it possible for a

7. The numbers that appear in this section are taken from the labor force projections in BLS 1997.

large number of jobs to be performed at home. A significant segment of the workforce should be able to work at least a portion of the time out of their homes and in that way enjoy more flexible hours and a more relaxed work environment. Many people, and particularly many families with young children, may view this change as an enormous benefit.

The Downside to the Next Century

Developments in technology will offer enormous opportunities to the people living and working in the first decades of the next century, but the picture will, of course, not be entirely positive. Many problems confronting the nation at present will grow far worse if not addressed in the near future.

The most important of these is the trend toward increasing inequality. Since the end of the 1970s the distribution of wealth and income has become increasingly unequal, producing a small number of winners (approximately 20 percent of the population) and a large number of losers. Even among the winners, the gains have been concentrated among those at the very top. In the 30 years before the 1970s, the gains from growth were relatively evenly spread, with the poorest making the biggest gains.

The factors behind this increase in inequality include international trade, declines in unionization rates, and the deregulation of many sectors of the economy. It will be difficult to reverse these and other changes in the decades to come, and so it is possible that wealth and income will continue to shift upward. And while 35 years of stagnant or declining incomes imply enormous economic strains for many families, the social strains may be far worse. Crime and disaffection from the political system are likely to increase enormously if the trend toward greater inequality continues over the next 35 years, and the response from the government may be greater repression. (The number of people in prisons and jails has nearly quadrupled over the last two decades; at that rate the United States will have more than 11 million people in jail by the year 2030.) If this is the world that we pass on to our children and grandchildren, then they will have considerable cause for complaint.

The health care system also presents enormous problems. If health care costs continue to grow as they have, at a rate significantly above the overall rate of inflation, then a larger and larger portion of the population will be unable to afford regular access to health care. Forty million Americans are without health insurance today, and this number could double or even triple by 2030 if health care costs grow at the rate projected by the Health Care

Financing Administration. At that point, close to half of the population may be dependent on Medicaid-type programs or private charity to provide them with emergency health care. The United States is alone among industrialized countries in its failure to provide health insurance to its citizens and to bring the growth of health costs under control. Continuing on this path for another 35 years will have disastrous consequences for large segments of the population.

Finally, the nation and the world are beset with serious environmental problems, the most significant of which is global warming. Projections suggest that the world may see substantial climatic disruptions by 2030—including higher water levels from the melting of the polar ice caps, more frequent and severe storms, and the destruction of fragile ecosystems across the planet—as a result of the buildup of greenhouse gases since preindustrial times. Since there is a long lead time between the emission of greenhouse gases and their effect on the weather, we have limited ability to prevent the damage that will occur between now and 2030. But if the country and the world do not move soon to a path of lower emissions, then we may be guaranteeing an environmental disaster later in the century. The potential destruction of the planet makes the prospect of higher Social Security taxes seem relatively minor.

Fix the Problems, Not Social Security

Due to the growth of the economy and improvements in technology, our children and grandchildren should be living much better lives materially in the years from 2020 to 2030 than we do at present, even if the pessimistic growth projections in the trustees' report prove accurate. The situation could even be far better than projected, for a variety of reasons: a high demand for labor, healthier and safer jobs, and healthier and longer lives. It could also be worse, marked by extreme gaps of wealth and poverty, a bankrupt health care system, and environmental catastrophe. If the country cannot deal with these more serious problems because it is diverted by debates over Social Security, then future generations will pay a tremendous price.

9 | An Honest Debate

WE ARE CURRENTLY in the midst of a major national debate over the future of Social Security, a kind of debate we have not seen since the 1930s. No one should be deceived as to its nature and significance.

It is not about shoring up the program's finances or how we can, as President Clinton put it, "save Social Security for the twenty-first century."[1] It is not about preparing for the retirement of the baby boom generation, which we have already done. And it is not about making the program more equitable or fair or improving it in any way. At its best, this debate is about how to cut Social Security. At its worst, it is about privatization, about undermining or even destroying the program that has formed the bedrock of the social safety net for more than half a century.

There are of course significant differences between the various proposals for "reform" that have been put forth. Privatization would have more serious consequences than some of the smaller proposed benefit cuts. But the cuts in benefits—whether packaged as an adjustment to the consumer price index (CPI), an increase in the retirement age, or changes in the formula for computing benefits—would cause a great deal of unnecessary pain and suffering among the elderly. The poorest among the elderly would be the hardest hit. These cuts, if enacted, would eventually push millions of senior citizens below the poverty line.

As we have seen, there is no defensible economic, actuarial, or demographic rationale for accepting these cuts, nor for privatization. In fact, the parameters of the entire debate should be rejected. While it is true that not all

1. President William Jefferson Clinton's radio address to the nation, March 21, 1998.

of the participants in the current debate hope to privatize or cut the program as much as politics will allow, and while some look favorably on the program and would like to preserve it, no one should confuse the present discussion with an honest one.

The fundamental premise on which the debate rests—that there is a legitimate reason for Americans to be concerned with the financial health of Social Security—is simply false. The fact that the trustees' intermediate-cost projections show a shortfall of less than 1 percent of gross domestic product over the long 75-year planning period is hardly worthy of the attention it has received. Indeed, it would scarcely be noticed if not for the array of political forces that have decided that the time is finally ripe to touch the "third rail" of American politics.

An unquestioned assumption in the debate is that no one's taxes can ever be raised, no matter how high the nation's future income rises, in order to keep the program's commitments. This limitation by itself should lead even the most credulous observer to question whether those who have framed this discussion are really interested in "fixing" Social Security.

How have we reached this sad state of affairs, in which those who would throw millions of senior citizens into poverty and undermine the retirement security of all future generations have come to be regarded as courageous leaders, bold defenders of the national interest from the special interests of politics? Historians looking back on this period may well marvel at how we managed to regress from the War on Poverty to the war against the poor, the old, the sick, and the bottom half of the working population generally.

Little more than 30 years ago we had leaders with a very different mission, a vastly different vision of American society and its potential. "The curse of poverty has no justification in our age," said Dr. Martin Luther King Jr. "It is socially as cruel and blind as the practice of cannibalism at the dawn of civilization. . . The time has come for us to civilize ourselves by the total, direct, and immediate abolition of poverty" (King 1967). King was of course exceptional, and even prophetic. He saw that rising military spending would crowd out programs for the alleviation of poverty, "that America would never invest the necessary funds or energies in rehabilitation of its poor so long as adventures like Vietnam continued to draw men and skills and money like some demonic destructive suction tube."[2] But even the architects of the Viet-

2. "A Time to Break Silence," speech by Martin Luther King Jr. at a meeting of

An Honest Debate

nam War had a domestic political agenda that was, at least in principle, radically different from today's bipartisan consensus.

"There are millions of Americans—one-fifth of our people—who have not shared in the abundance which has been granted to most of us, and on whom the gates of opportunity have been closed," said President Johnson in 1964, as he called upon Americans "to declare war on a domestic enemy which threatens the strength of our nation and the welfare of the people." That enemy was poverty—not welfare, entitlement spending, or the national debt. "Today for the first time in all the history of the human race, a great nation is able to make and is willing to make a commitment to eradicate poverty among its people."[3]

What a shock it would be to hear such words today from an American president, or even a serious candidate for the office, as the twentieth century draws to a close. Instead we are admonished about the commitments we can no longer afford to keep. In the words of President Clinton, "Nearly everybody knows that something substantial, really substantial, has to be done to reform the Social Security system to accommodate the baby boom generation and then, subsequent, the generations after that."[4]

Paying down the national debt is also given a high priority, although there is no economic research that can show any but the most trivial potential gains from such a policy. We entered the 1960s with a debt that was 46 percent of our economy, the same as it is today (50 years ago it was 84 percent) (*ERP* 1998, table B-79). Yet few were worried that this debt would choke off growth, and it did not.

Our real income per person is 71 percent higher than it was 30 years ago (*ERP* 1998, table B-31), yet we are told that we cannot afford to honor our social contract with the elderly and, especially, the poor, who just lost a 63-year-old federal entitlement: Aid to Families with Dependent Children. Meanwhile the balanced budget agreement of 1997 made sure that those who had doubled their wealth in the stock market in the course of three years would get a generous tax break when they cashed in their winnings. Again there was

---

Concerned Clergy and Laity, New York, April 4, 1967.

3. Remarks by President Lyndon B. Johnson on the War on Poverty, March 16, 1964.

4. Remarks by President William Jefferson Clinton on the report of the Social Security and Medicare trustees, April 28, 1998. See the *New York Daily News*, "Brief Reprieve for Medicare, Social Security," April 29, 1998.

no economic analysis to indicate that the rest of society would benefit from this policy, as the Clinton administration acknowledged before signing the bill into law.

Social Security has always had its opponents, as has Medicare (enacted in 1965). But historically this opposition has come from the right side of the political spectrum. Barry Goldwater's crushing defeat in the presidential election of 1964 sent a message to conservatives that the programs of the New Deal still enjoyed firm support among the electorate. The architects of the New Right, which captured the Republican Party and the presidency 16 years later, took this lesson to heart and set about building their constituency primarily on the basis of social issues such as abortion and school prayer. Campaigns for lower taxes (such as California's famous Proposition 13 in the 1970s) were also important, but going after Social Security was one risk that never seemed worth taking. But conservative opponents have gotten bolder, and what distinguishes the present period is that so many liberals have signed on to one or another of the attacks on Social Security. This is explainable in part, perhaps, by the devolution of liberalism and its leadership. But another piece of the puzzle has to do with the recasting of the arguments about Social Security in more technical and mystifying forms.

The debate over the accuracy of the CPI, for example, is presented as a technical issue, when in fact it is about cutting Social Security's cost-of-living increases. Advocates of privatization have staked out their turf on the technical terrain of "rates of return," alleging (inaccurately, as we have seen) that the stock market offers a better deal. And of course the greatest of all mystifications is the demographic determinism—that ever-menacing "age wave"—that serves as the foundation, however tenuous, for the entire structure of attacks on entitlements for the elderly. In an age in which biodeterminism generally has supplanted so much of the search for the social causes of humanity's problems, this particular ideology has a ready and credulous audience.

This mystification has helped to convince prominent liberals to join the ranks of the entitlement cutters, and even in some cases to support partial privatization. Of course, not all of the arguments that threaten Social Security at this juncture are put forth in technical or confusing forms. The traditional libertarian position remains well represented among the privatizers, and an appeal is made to an ethos of selfishness, which stands diametrically opposed to the principles of social insurance. But such an appeal has never been able to galvanize much support among the general public. Few Americans believe that those who were not able to save enough for their retirement or were not fortunate enough to have been covered by a private pension plan should be abandoned in their old age. Social Security's opponents could never have gotten so far, and so close to destroying the foundations of the program, without the technical arguments of the liberal entitlement cutters.

The most farsighted of Social Security's conservative opponents have recognized in privatization the opportunity for social engineering on a grand scale. The number of households owning stock, especially through retirement savings deposited in mutual funds, has risen dramatically over the last decade. But they remain a minority at 41 percent, with most holdings relatively small and most of the wealth highly concentrated in the richest households (Kennickell, Starr-McCluer, and Sunden 1997). The establishment of individual accounts out of Social Security taxes for 140 million Americans would constitute an enormous broadening of stock ownership.

For the social engineers in the privatization camp, such a move is valued for its potential to expand the proportion of people who identify more as stockholders than as employees and see their fortunes as tied to the profits of the corporate sector. These privatizers see some precedent for their hopes in the birth of a large class of homeowners after World War II, spurred on by the federal government's creation of the home mortgage income tax deduction (Glassman 1997).

The privatization, or even weakening, of Social Security would indeed be a big step toward transforming the ethics of our political culture. It would bring us closer to molding the "neoclassical man," the atomistic individual who is the building block of the abstract models of modern microeconomics. This person's economic interactions with others are based on relationships of exchange, mediated through markets, and devoid of any common bond that one shares with the rest of society.

Social insurance is based on a fundamentally different set of principles. Its starting point is that "we are all in this together" and therefore have a shared obligation to provide security for everyone against the hazards of old age, disability, sickness, or injury. Coverage is universal, and therefore so are contributions—in the case of Social Security, for example, mandatory for all employed persons. The social nature of this compact, in addition to the insurance aspects of it, means that the "returns" on contributions are not directly comparable to those of an individual investing her savings in the stock market. Social Security is not a mutual fund set up to maximize the returns of its subscribers, nor was it ever intended to be.

As it turns out, social insurance is also many times more efficient than private insurance for protecting against the same set of risks. We need more social insurance, not less, because it works. As recently as 1959, 35 percent of senior citizens lived in poverty (SSA 1996b, 169). Thanks to Social Security, that number has been reduced to 11 percent today. Two-thirds of the elderly depend on the program for the majority of their income, and about half of the nation's senior citizens would be in poverty without it (SSA 1996b, 21).

Rather than cutting our nation's largest and most successful antipoverty program, we should extend the principles of universal social insurance to the area of health care. Medicare and Medicaid have taken us part of the way, but the continued and now growing reliance on private insurance and market-driven solutions has left us with the most expensive health care system in the developed world, and the only one that leaves tens of millions of its citizens without coverage. Other industrialized countries have managed to care for a rising proportion of elderly without facing uncontrollable health care costs. There is no reason that we cannot do the same, and social insurance holds the best promise of correcting the real, nondemographic causes of our "entitlements crisis" in the area of health care.

But first we must free ourselves from the generational warriors and their accountants, the privatizers, and all the "reformers" who have hauled Social Security halfway to the chopping block. As we have seen, there is no logical or economic basis for their attempts to pit the young against the old or the healthy against the sick. Even at the slow rates of economic growth forecast by Social Security's actuaries, our economy will produce more than enough to provide a comfortable retirement for the elderly. At the same time, there will be enough for a steady and sizable rise in the income of the working population—before, during, and after the retirement of the baby boom generation.

If we feel a need to have the Social Security accounts balanced over a 75-year time horizon, that is a simple enough task to accomplish. President Clinton's proposal to put $2,800 billion of general revenue into the trust fund over the next 15 years eliminates almost half the projected shortfall. Raising the cap on wage earnings subject to the Security Security payroll tax, to offset the impact that increasing wage inequality has had on the trust fund, would eliminate more than half of the remaining gap. The rest of the shortfall could be eliminated by some combination of additional general revenues and increasing the trust fund's yield by allowing it to purchase government guaranteed bonds, such as those issued by the Federal National Mortgage Association.

The point here is not to prescribe the exact path by which future obligations to retirees will be met. This will be determined by future generations of voters, regardless of the legislative changes that we might make today. The point is simply to show that it is easy to describe a solution that does not imply serious pain for either retirees or workers, present or future generations. The real clouds on the long-term economic horizon have little to do with demographic changes or government programs for the elderly. We are threatened instead by our apparent inability to contain the inflation generated by the private health care sector. And, most importantly, we have a serious problem of income distribution that has left the majority of the labor force with nothing to show for the last two decades of economic growth. This unprecedented trend toward inequality, if it continues into the future, will indeed create serious social problems and possibly even unrest.

But these are the issues that our political leaders have chosen to ignore. They have found it easier to blame the inexorable, unseen forces of demographic change than to point the finger at powerful insurers profiting from Medicare and the health care system generally. They have also found it easier to talk about the nation getting older than about the rich getting richer.

Until the myths of intergenerational conflict, demographic determinism, and runaway entitlement spending have been dispelled, there is no point in talking about the "reform" of Social Security. There is nothing to be gained, and everything to be lost, in a policy debate whose conclusion is predetermined by a set of false constraints and beliefs. In such a situation the best that can be hoped for is to bury the issue, and bury it deep. We can dig it up later, when the elderly are portrayed not as a threat to the well-being of future generations but as fellow human beings whose efforts and sacrifices helped build the foundation for the material wealth we enjoy today. Then we can have an honest public debate about the future of social insurance.

Appendix

The Feldstein-Samwick Plan

In the spring of 1998, Martin Feldstein, president of the National Bureau of Economic Research and formerly the chief economist in the Reagan administration, along with Dartmouth professor Andrew Samwick, proposed a new plan for partially privatizing Social Security. It required neither benefit cuts nor tax increases and partly for this reason attracted considerable interest from political circles.

While many of the details of the plan remain to be worked out, the basic proposition involves using the budget surplus to create private accounts equal to 2.0 percent of each worker's wages. Workers will then manage these accounts through their working lives and draw on them in retirement as a supplement to their regular Social Security benefit. The savings to the Social Security system result from the fact that the standard benefit will be reduced by 75 percent of the amount of money taken from the private account. For example, if a worker's private account yields an income of $1,000 a year, then his or her Social Security benefit will be reduced by $750 a year. This saves the Social Security fund $750 a year while at the same time guaranteeing the worker a benefit that is at least as large as what he or she would receive under the current system.

Several serious problems with the Feldstein-Samwick plan can be identified, some of which are common to any privatization proposal and some of which are unique to this plan. First, in terms of administration, the plan does not specify whether the accounts will be centrally managed, along the lines of the federal government's Thrift Savings Plan for federal employees, or be administered in a decentralized manner, as are the Chilean and British systems. On the former route the costs can be relatively low, although still substantial (see EBRI 1998b). However, in a centrally administered system the federal government can easily apply political criteria to investment decisions, a concern that Feldstein has expressed with reference to direct government investment of the trust fund. If the accounts are administered in a decentralized manner, then the costs are likely to be prohibitive, ensuring that many low-wage workers receive negative returns on their money. Even after five years, workers who earn $10,000 a year will have accumulated just $1,000 in their accounts under this system. If an account earns an annual return of 4.0 percent before expenses, the return would be negative even if the expenses were as low as $3.50 per month. Tens of millions of workers would find themselves in this situation.

The proposal also does not specify whether it would require annuitization of the accounts upon retirement. Annuitization in this plan poses the same problem as with other proposals. If it is not required, then the problem of adverse selection will make annuities extremely expensive for those with average life expectancies. If it is required, then it creates the appearance of unfairness, as people with short life expectancies (e.g., terminal cancer patients) will be required to surrender a lifetime of savings for virtually no benefit.

These issues arise with any privatization plan. However, with the Feldstein-Samwick plan, not requiring annuitization creates the additional problem of encouraging gaming of the system. If workers annuitize, they lose 75 percent of any benefits they draw from their accounts by having this amount deducted from their regular Social Security benefits. But if they opt not to annuitize their individual accounts and do not draw upon them, they receive their full Social Security benefits. In effect, there is a 75 percent tax rate on any money taken from the individual accounts, providing retirees with a strong disincentive to spend money from these accounts. Certainly anyone with savings outside their accounts would spend that money first, before drawing down his or her individual account. In general, most higher-paid workers would be able to accomplish this without much difficulty, which means that the individual accounts simply end up increasing the inheritances of the children of well-paid workers.

However, it is also likely that most middle-income workers would be able to avoid drawing on their individual accounts as well. While relatively few middle-income workers have accumulated substantial savings by their retirement, most do own a home, and these workers would benefit enormously by mortgaging their houses to avoid having to pay the 75 percent tax on withdrawals from their individual accounts. A further option available to many middle-income retirees would be to borrow money from their children. Since $10,000 in an individual account is worth only $2,500 to retired workers, they could borrow this $2,500 from their children and repay them with the full $10,000 at death.

In short, the only people who are not likely to be able to game the Feldstein-Samwick plan are lower-income people who lack any significant assets, including a home, and who do not have children who can afford to lend them money to support their retirement. Under this scenario, the plan ends up being extremely regressive, since it increases the bequests of middle- and upper-income people while giving almost nothing to lower-income workers. It also provides virtually no savings for the Social Security system, since only the poorest beneficiaries end up drawing on their individual accounts and having a corresponding reduction in benefits. In short, the Feldstein-Samwick plan without mandatory annuitization is simply a large tax break for middle- and upper-income workers that has little effect on the solvency of the Social Security program.

The other feature of the Feldstein-Samwick plan that distinguishes it from other proposals is that it actually *increases* the benefits received by retirees. The projected budget surpluses, which could be used for education, child care, or other expenditures that benefit children, will instead be used to enlarge the retirement benefits that the government guarantees workers. This is ironic, since the entry point to the debate over the future of Social Security was the supposed generational injustice implied by the current pattern of benefits and taxes. Generational inequity, if it exists now, will only get worse if we implement this plan. It is remarkable that political figures who have spoken solemnly about this alleged injustice would even consider the Feldstein-Samwick plan.

If the political consensus views an increase in retiree benefits as desirable, then we can accomplish this goal in a much more progressive and efficient manner than proposed by Feldstein and Samwick. Their proposal in effect uses general tax revenue to offset the projected shortfall in the Social Security trust fund and increases the amount being paid out to Social Security beneficiaries by 0.5 percentage points of covered payroll (25 percent of the 2.0 percentage points placed in individual accounts). Instead of creating a complex system of individual accounts, however, the same money from general tax revenue could be used to support the trust fund and increase the size of current benefit payments to retirees. The additional money could simply be added to the benefits retirees currently receive. The sum proposed by Feldstein and Samwick would be sufficient to allow an increase in annual benefit payments of approximately 5.0 percent for each retiree. Alternatively, the increase could be delayed for a number of years to allow the trust fund to accumulate interest or stock returns from investing the money. This step would eventually allow for a larger increase in benefits.

Such a plan would have exactly the same effect on the solvency of the trust fund as the Feldstein-Samwick plan, and it would distribute the increase in benefits in a much more progressive manner. Since the current payback structure is highly progressive, lower-income workers would receive far more under this system than under the Feldstein-Samwick plan. For example, a worker whose earnings averaged $10,000 per year would get approximately $25 more per month if current benefits are increased just 5.0 percent. Alternatively, delaying the increase for 10 years would increase the extra benefits to approximately $40 per month (in today's dollars). Using optimistic assumptions about administrative costs and returns, even after 30 years such a worker would see an increase in benefits of only about $15 a month under the Feldstein-Samwick plan.

In addition to providing a more progressive payback structure, this policy of enhancing the current system would also allow for significant administrative savings. If the costs of individual accounts are $30 per year (certainly a low estimate given the existing research on the issue), then the cumulative savings from expanding the existing system rather than adopting the Feldstein-Samwick plan will be more than $50 billion over the next 10 years. We could use this money on education or child care or to meet any other need that has been neglected in recent years. Under the Feldstein-Samwick plan, this money is simply wasted in administrative expenses.

Finally, a subtext to the Feldstein-Samwick plan may threaten the long-term health of Social Security. Under the plan, individuals will keep the full amount from their individual accounts, but money will be deducted from the Social Security benefit. For many people, particularly higher-income workers, it might appear that the individual accounts are providing a very good return while the Social Security system is providing virtually nothing. If the point is to devise a way to undermine political support for the existing Social Security system, it would be hard to find a better mechanism than the Feldstein-Samwick plan.

References

Advisory Council on Social Security. 1997. *Report of the 1994–96 Advisory Council on Social Security.* Vol. 1. Washington, D.C.: Advisory Council on Social Security.

————. 1997. *Report of the 1994–95 Advisory Council on Social Security.* Vol. 2, *Reports of the Technical Panel on Trends and Issues in Retirement Savings and Presentations to the Council.* Washington, D.C.: Advisory Council on Social Security.

Aizcorbe, A. M., and P. C. Jackman. 1993. "The Commodity Substitution Effect in CPI Data, 1982–91." *Monthly Labor Review,* December, pp. 25–33.

————. 1997. Update of "The Commodity Substitution Effect in CPI Data, 1982–91." Unpublished data prepared for Senate Finance Committee Advisory Commission to Study the Consumer Price Index. Washington, D.C.: Bureau of Labor Statistics.

Auerbach, A. J., J. Gokhale, and L. J. Kotlikoff. 1991. "Generational Accounts: A Meaningful Alternative to the Deficit Accounting." In D. Bradford, ed., *Tax Policy and the Economy.* Cambridge, Mass.: MIT Press.

Auerbach, A. J., J. Gokhale, L. J. Kotlikoff, and E. Steigum Jr. 1993. *Generational Accounting in Norway: Is Norway Overconsuming Its Petroleum Wealth?* Ruth Pollack Working Paper Series on Economics, no. 24. Boston, Mass.: Boston University, Department of Economics.

Baker, D. 1995. *Robbing the Cradle? A Critical Assessment of Generational Accounting.* Washington, D.C.: Economic Policy Institute.

————. 1996. *Getting Prices Right: A Methodologically Consistent Consumer Price Index, 1953–94.* Washington, D.C.: Economic Policy Institute.

————. 1997. *Getting Prices Right: The Debate over the Consumer Price Index.* Armonk, N.Y.: M. E. Sharpe.

————. 1998. *Defusing the Baby Boomer Time Bomb: Projections of Income in the 21st Century.* Washington, D.C.: Economic Policy Institute.

Ball, R. M. 1998. "A Commentary on the Current Social Security Debate." Founding Chair of the Board, National Academy of Social Insurance. Typescript.

Ball, R. M., E. U. Fierst, G. T. Johnson, T. W. Jones, G. Kourpias, and G. M. Shea. 1997. "Social Security for the 21st Century: A Strategy to Maintain Benefits and Strengthen America's Family Protection Plan." Washington, D.C.: Social Security Administration (www.ssa.gov).

Barth, J. R., G. Iden, F. S. Russek, and M. Wohar. 1991. "The Effects of Federal Budget

References

Deficits on Interest Rates and the Composition of Output." In R. G. Penner, ed., *The Great Fiscal Experiment*. Washington, D.C.: Urban Institute.

Beach, W.M., and G.G. Davis. 1998. *Social Security's Rate of Return*. Washington, D.C.: Heritage Foundation.

Bellandi, D. 1997. "Fed's Fraud Cases Boom in '90s." *Modern Healthcare*, August 18, p. 10.

Bennet, J. 1997. "Congress 'Time-Bomb' Tax Cuts Criticized." *San Diego Union-Tribune*, July 1, p. A1.

Bosworth, B., G. Burtless, and J. Sabelhaus. 1991. "The Decline in Saving: Some Microeconomic Evidence." *Brookings Papers on Economic Activity*, pp. 183–256.

Brown, M. L., L. G. Kessler, and F. G. Reuter. 1990. "Is the Supply of Mammography Machines Outstripping Need and Demand?" *Annals of Internal Medicine*, October 1, p. 547.

Bureau of Labor Statistics (BLS). 1997. "Industry Output and Employment Projections to 2006." *Monthly Labor Review* 120, no. 11, p. 44.

———. 1998a. "Employee Tenure in 1998." Supplement to the *Current Population Survey*. Washington, D.C.: BLS.

———. 1998b. "Employment Situation." News release, October.

Burman, L., R. Penner, G. Steuerle, E. Toder, M. Moon, L. Thompson, M. Weisner, and A. Carasso. 1998. *Policy Challenges Posed by the Aging of America*. Washington, D.C.: Urban Institute.

Carroll, C., and L. H. Summers. 1989. *Consumption Growth Parallels Income Growth: Some New Evidence*. Working Paper no. 3090. Cambridge, Mass.: National Bureau of Economic Research.

Carter, M. N., and W. G. Shipman. 1996. *Promises to Keep: Saving Social Security's Dream*. Washington, D.C.: Regenery Press.

Census Bureau. 1996. *Current Population Survey*. Washington, D.C.: Census Bureau.

———. 1997. *Current Population Survey: Income 1997*. Washington, D.C.: Census Bureau.

Centers for Disease Control and Prevention/National Center for Health Statistics (CDCP/NCHS). 1993. *Vital Statistics of the United States, 1993, Life Tables*. Atlanta, Ga.: CDCP.

———. 1997. *Monthly Vital Statistics Report* 45, no. 11(S)2, June 12, p. 19.

Chirinko, R. S. 1993. "Business Fixed Investment Spending: A Critical Survey of Modeling Strategies, Empirical Results, and Policy Implications." *Journal of Economic Literature* 31, pp. 1875–1911.

Congressional Budget Office (CBO). 1993. *Economic and Budget Outlook: Fiscal Years 1993–1998*. Washington, D.C.: U.S. Government Printing Office.

———. 1994. *Economic and Budget Outlook: An Update, September 1994*. Washington, D.C.: U.S. Government Printing Office.

———. 1995. *Who Pays and When? An Assessment of Generational Accounting*. Washington, D.C.: U.S. Government Printing Office.

References

———. 1996. *Economic and Budget Outlook: Fiscal Years 1997–2006*. Washington, D.C.: U.S. Government Printing Office.

———. 1998. *Economic and Budget Outlook: Fiscal Years 1999–2008*. Washington, D.C.: U.S. Government Printing Office.

Corporate Research Group. 1997. *The Outlook for Managed Care: An Industry Forecast*. New Rochelle, N.Y.: Corporate Research Group.

Crandall, R., and J. Ellig. 1996. *Economic Deregulation and Customer Choice: Lessons for the Electric Industry*. Fairfax, Va.: Center for Market Processes.

Cutler, D. M. 1994. Review of *Generational Accounting: Knowing Who Pays, and When, for What We Spend*, by L. J. Kotlikoff. *National Tax Journal*, winter, pp. 61–67.

———. 1996. *Public Policy for Health Care*, Working Paper no. 5591. Cambridge, Mass.: National Bureau of Economic Research.

Cutler, D.M., and B.C. Madrian. 1996. *Labor Market Responses to Rising Health Insurance Costs: Evidence on Hours Worked*, Working Paper no. 5525. Cambridge, Mass.: National Bureau of Economic Research.

Department of Commerce. 1997. *Statistical Abstract of the United States, 1997*. Washington, D.C.: U.S. Government Printing Office.

Economic Report of the President (ERP). 1998. Washington, D.C.: U.S. Government Printing Office.

Eisner, R. 1997. *The Great Deficit Scares*. New York: Century Foundation Press.

Employee Benefit Research Institute (EBRI). 1997. *Trends in Health Insurance Coverage*. Issue Brief no. 185. Washington, D.C.: EBRI.

———. 1998a. *How Do Individual Accounts Stack Up? An Evaluation Using the EBRI-SSASIM2 Policy Simulation Model*. Washington, D.C.: EBRI.

———. 1998b. *Individual Social Security Accounts: Issues in Assessing Administrative Feasibility and Costs*. Special Report SR-34. Washington, D.C.: EBRI.

Engen, E., W. Gale, and J. K. Scholz. 1996. "The Illusory Effect of Saving Incentives on Saving." *Journal of Economic Perspectives* 10, fall, pp. 113–38.

Fazzari, S. M. 1993. *Investment and U.S. Fiscal Policy in the 1990s*. Washington, D.C.: Economic Policy Institute.

Feldstein, M. 1974. "Social Security, Induced Retirement and Aggregate Capital Accumulation." *Journal of Political Economy* 82, no. 5, pp. 905–26.

———. 1995. *Social Security and Saving: New Time Series Evidence*. Working Paper no. 5054. Cambridge, Mass.: National Bureau of Economic Research.

Feldstein, M., and A. Samwick. 1997. *The Economics of Prefunding Social Security and Medicare*. Working Paper no. 6055. Cambridge, Mass.: National Bureau of Economic Research.

———. 1998. *Two Percent Personal Retirement Accounts: Their Potential Effects on Social Security Tax Rates and National Saving*. Working Paper no. 6540. Cambridge, Mass.: National Bureau of Economic Research.

Freeman, R. 1996. "Solving the New Inequality." *Boston Review* 21, no. 6.

Freudenheim, M. 1998. "Health Insurers Seek Big Increases in Their Premiums." *New York Times*, April 24, p. A1.

References

Fries, J. F. 1989. "The Compression of Morbidity: Near or Far?" *Milbank Quarterly* 67, no. 2, pp. 208–231.

Fries, J. F., C. E. Koop, J. Sokolov, C. E. Beadle, and D. Wright. 1998. "Beyond Health Promotion: Reducing Need and Demand for Medical Care." *Health Affairs* 17, no. 2, p. 70–84.

General Accounting Office (GAO). 1991. *Canadian Health Insurance: Lessons for the United States*. Report to the Chairman, Committee on Government Operations, House of Representatives, Washington, D.C.

Getzen, T. 1992. "Population Aging and the Growth of Health Expenditures." *Journal of Gerontology* 47, no. 3, pp. S98–S104.

Glassman, J. K. 1997. "Do-It-Yourself Retirement Plans." *Washington Post*, January 21, p. A11.

Goldschlag, William. 1998. "Brief Reprieve for Medicare, Social Security." *New York Daily News*, April 29, p. 4.

Goode, R., and C. E. Steurele. 1994. "Generational Accounts and Fiscal Policy." *Tax Notes* 65, no. 8, pp. 1027–32.

Gordon, R. 1990a. *The Measurement of Durable Goods Prices*. Chicago: University of Chicago Press.

———. 1990b. "What Is New-Keynesian Economics?" *Journal of Economic Literature*, September, pp. 1115–71.

Griliches, Z., and I. Cockburn. 1994. "Generics and New Goods in Pharmaceutical Indexes." *American Economic Review*, December, pp. 1213–32.

Haveman, R. 1994. "Should Generational Accounts Replace Public Budgets and Deficits?" *Journal of Economic Perspectives* 8, no. 1, pp. 95–111.

Health Care Financing Administration (HCFA). 1997a. *Financial Report, Fiscal Year 1997*. Washington, D.C.: HCFA.

———. 1997b. *Health Care Financing Review, Statistical Supplement, 1997*. Washington, D.C.: HCFA.

Hilzenrath, D. S. 1997. "Bold Scams Bilk Medicare of Billions." *Washington Post*, August 8, p. A1.

House, J. S., R. Kessler, A. R. Herzog, et al. 1990. "Age, Socioeconomic Status, and Health." *Milbank Quarterly* 68, no. 3, pp. 383–411.

Iams, H. 1993. "Earnings of Couples: A Cohort Analysis." *Social Security Bulletin* 56, no. 3, pp. 22–32.

Jorgenson, D., and D. Slesnick. 1983. "Individual and Social Cost-of-Living Indexes." In W. Diewert and C. Montmarquette, eds., *Price Level Measurement*. Ottawa: Statistics Canada.

Kennickell, A. B., M. Starr-McCluer, and A. E. Sunden. 1997. "Family Finances in the U.S.: Recent Evidence from the Survey of Consumer Finances." *Federal Reserve Bulletin* 83, p. 1.

King, M. L., Jr. 1967. *Where Do We Go from Here? Chaos or Community?* New York: Harper and Row.

References

Kotlikoff, L. J. 1993. *Generational Accounting: Knowing Who Pays, and When, for What We Spend*. New York: Free Press.

Kotlikoff, L. J., and J. Sachs. 1997. "Privatizing Social Security: It's High Time to Privatize." *Brookings Review* 15, summer, pp. 16–23.

Krugman, P. 1996a. "Demographics and Destiny." *New York Times*, October 20, sec. 7, p. 12.

———. 1996b. "Who's the Real Economist?" *Slate*, November 11 (www.slate.com).

Kurtz, H. 1998. "Democrats Chase Votes with a Safety Net." *Washington Post*, October 28, p. A4.

Lakonishok, J., A. Shleifer, and R. W. Vishny. 1992. "The Structure and Performance of the Money Management Industry." *Brookings Papers on Economic Activity (Microeconomics)*, pp. 339–79.

Leone, R. C. 1997. "Why Boomers Don't Spell Bust." *American Prospect*, January/February, no. 30, pp. 68–72.

Levit, K. R, H. C. Lazenby, B. R. Braden, et al. 1996. "National Health Expenditures, 1994." *Health Care Financing Review* 17, no. 3, p. 205.

Levit, K. R., H. C. Lazenby, B. R. Braden, and National Health Accounts Team. 1998. "National Health Spending Trends in 1996." *Health Affairs* 17, no. 1, pp. 35–51.

Lieberman, T. 1997. "Social Insecurity: The Campaign to Take the System Private." *Nation*, January 27, pp. 11–18.

Light, D. W. 1994. "Managed Care: False and Real Solutions." *Lancet*, October 29, pp. 1197-99.

Lubitz, J., J. Beebe, and C. Baker. 1995. "Longevity and Medicare Expenditures." *New England Journal of Medicine* 332, no. 15, pp. 999-1003.

Madrian, B. C. 1994. "Employment-Based Health Insurance and Job Mobility: Is There Evidence of Job-Lock?" *Quarterly Journal of Economics* 109, no. 1, pp. 27-54.

Manton, K. G., L. Corder, and E. Stallard. 1997. "Chronic Disability Trends in Elderly United States Populations: 1982-1994." *Proceedings of the National Academy of Sciences* 94, no. 6, pp. 2593–98.

Marmor, T., and J. Oberlander. 1998. "Rethinking Medicare Reform." *Health Affairs* 17, no. 1, pp. 52–68.

Merck Family Fund. 1995. *Yearning for Balance*. Whitehouse Station, N.J.: Preuss.

Mishel, L., J. Bernstein, and J. Schmitt. 1997. *The State of Working America, 1997–98*. Economic Policy Institute Series. Armonk, N.Y.: M. E. Sharpe.

———. 1999. *The State of Working America, 1998–99*. An Economic Policy Institute Book. Ithaca, N.Y.: ILR Press.

Mitchell, A. 1998. "Election Year May Make Social Security Too Hot to Handle." *New York Times*, April 21, p. A17.

Mitchell, O. S. 1996. *Administrative Costs in Public and Private Pension Systems*. Working Paper no. 5734. Cambridge, Mass.: National Bureau of Economic Research.

Mitchell, O. S., J. M. Poterba, and M. J. Warshawsky. 1997. *New Evidence on the Money's Worth of Individual Annuities*. Working Paper no. 6002. Cambridge, Mass.: National Bureau of Economic Research.

References

Moon, M., C. Kuntz, and L. Pounder. 1996. *Protecting Low Income Medicare Beneficiaries*. Washington, D.C.: Urban Institute.

Morgan, R. O., B. A. Virnig, C. A. DeVito, and N. A. Persily. 1997. "The Medicare-HMO Revolving Door: The Healthy Go In and the Sick Go Out." *New England Journal of Medicine* 337, no. 3, pp. 169–175.

Moulton, B. R., and K. E. Moses. 1997. *Addressing Quality Change in the Consumer Price Index*. Working Paper no. 304. Washington, D.C.: Bureau of Labor Statistics.

National Center for Education Statistics. 1996. *Digest of Education Statistics, 1996*. Washington, D.C.: U.S. Government Printing Office.

Navarro, V. 1990. "Race or Class versus Race and Class: Mortality Differentials in the United States." *Lancet*, no. 2, pp. 1238–40.

Nelson, L., R. S. Brown, M. Gold, A. Ciemnecki, and E. Docteur. 1997. "Access to Care in Medicare HMOs, 1996." *Health Affairs* 16, no. 2, pp. 148–156.

New Orleans Times-Picayune. 1998. "Medicare Trust Fund Needs More Work, Officials Say." August 13, p. A6.

New York Times. 1988. "Poll Finds Americans Are Ignorant of Science." October 25, p. A10.

Office of Management and Budget (OMB). 1992–94. *Budget of the United States Government, Analytical Perspectives*. Washington, D.C.: U.S. Government Printing Office.

———. 1994. *Budget of the United States Government, Analytical Perspectives, Fiscal Year 1995*. Washington, D.C.: U.S. Government Printing Office.

Organization for Economic Cooperation and Development (OECD). 1997. *Health Care Data, 1997*. Geneva: OECD.

Passell, P. 1997. "Some Experts Say Inflation Is Understated." *New York Times*, November 6, p. D1.

Pear, R. 1998. "New Health Plans Due for Elderly." *New York Times*, June 10, p. A1.

Peterson, P. G. 1996. *Will America Grow Up before It Grows Old?* New York: Random House.

Poterba, J. M. 1997. *The Rate of Return to Corporate Capital and Factor Shares: New Estimates Using Revised National Income Accounts and Capital Stock Data*. Working Paper no. 6263. Cambridge, Mass.: National Bureau of Economic Research.

Poterba, J. M., S. F. Venti, and D. A. Wise. 1996. "How Retirement Saving Programs Increase Saving." *Journal of Economic Perspectives* 10, no. 4, pp. 91–112.

Rasell, E. 1997. "Achieving Long-Term Medicare Financial Stability: A Universal Health Care System Is the Only Answer." Paper presented at the Health Care Consumer's Summit on the Future of Medicare and Universal Coverage, April 25–27, Washington, D.C.

Retchen, S. M., R. S. Brown, S. J. Yeh, D. Chu, and L. Moreno. 1997. "Outcomes of Stroke Patients in Medicare Fee for Service and Managed Care." *Journal of the American Medical Association* 278, no. 2, pp. 119–124.

Riley, G., C. Tudor, Y. Chiang, and M. Ingber. 1996. "Health Status of Medicare Enrollees in HMOs and Fee-for-Service in 1994." *Health Care Financing Review* 17, no. 4, pp. 65–76.

References

Rogot, E., P. D. Sorlie, and N. J. Johnson. 1992. "Life Expectancy by Employment Status, Income, and Education in the National Longitudinal Mortality Study." *Public Health Reports* 107, no. 4, pp. 457-461.

Saltman, R. B., and J. Figueras. 1998. "Analyzing the Evidence on European Health Care Reforms." *Health Affairs* 17, no. 2, pp. 85–108.

Schieber, G. J., J. Poullier, and L. M. Greenwald. 1993. "DataWatch: Health Spending, Delivery, and Outcomes in OECD Countries." *Health Affairs* 12, no. 2, p. 123.

Schmitt, J., and L. Mishel. 1998. *An Evaluation of the G7 Economies in the 1990s.* Technical Paper. Washington, D.C.: Economic Policy Institute.

Senate Finance Committee. 1996. *Toward a More Accurate Measure of the Cost of Living.* Final Report to the Senate Finance Committee from the Advisory Commission to Study the Consumer Price Index. 104th Congress, 2nd session.

Shaughnessey, P. W., R. E. Schlenker, and D. F. Hittle. 1994. "Home Health Care Outcomes under Capitated and Fee-for-Service Payment." *Health Care Financing Review* 16, no. 1, p. 187.

Social Security Administration (SSA). 1996a. *Annual Report of the Board of Trustees of the Federal Old-Age and Survivors Insurance and Disability Insurance Trust Funds.* Washington, D.C.: SSA.

———. 1996b. *Annual Statistical Supplement to the Social Security Bulletin.* Washington, D.C.: SSA.

———. 1997. *Annual Statistical Supplement to the Social Security Bulletin.* Table 3.E2. Washington, D.C.: SSA.

———. 1998a. *Social Security: Basic Facts.* Washington, D.C.: SSA.

———. 1998b. *Will Social Security Be There for You?* Publication no. 05-10055. Washington, D.C.: SSA.

———. 1999. *Annual Report of the Board of Trustees of the Federal Old-Age and Survivors Insurance and Disability Insurance Trust Funds.* Washington, D.C.: SSA.

Steinhauer, J. 1997. "What Ever Happened to Service?" *New York Times,* March 4, p. D1.

Steurele, C. E., and J. M. Bakija. 1994. *Retooling Social Security for the 21st Century: Right and Wrong Approaches.* Washington, D.C.: Urban Institute.

Stevenson, R. W. 1998a. "Bipartisan Plan for Rescue of Social Security Involves Markets and Retirement at 70." *New York Times,* May 19, p. A17.

———. 1998b. "Clinton Opens Campaign for Quick Action on Social Security." *New York Times,* February 10, p. A16.

———. 1998c. "Federal Reserve Cuts Rates Again: Wall St. Surges." *New York Times,* October 16, p. A1.

———. 1998d. "To Social Security Critics, the Argument Is Simple." *New York Times,* March 2, p. A1.

Thomas, L. B., and A. Abderrezak. 1988. "Anticipated Budget Deficits and the Term Structure of Interest Rates." *Southern Economic Journal,* July, pp. 150–161.

Thurow, L. 1996. "The Birth of a Revolutionary Class." *New York Times Magazine,* May 19.

References

Urban Institute. 1998. *Policy Changes Posed by the Aging of America.* Washington, D.C.: Urban Institute.

Vita, A. J., R. B. Terry, H. B. Hubert, and J. F. Fries. 1998. "Aging, Health Risks, and Cumulative Disability." *New England Journal of Medicine* 338, no. 15, pp. 1035–41.

Waidman, T. A. 1998. "Potential Effects of Raising Medicare's Eligibility Age." *Health Affairs* 17, no. 2, p. 156.

Waldo, D. R., S. T. Sonnefeld, J. A. Lemieux, and D. R. McKusick. 1991. "Health Spending Through 2030: Three Scenarios." *Health Affairs* 10, no. 4, pp. 231–42.

Waldo, D. R., S. T. Sonnefeld, D. R. McKusick, and R. H. Arnett III. 1989. "Health Care Financing Trends: Health Expenditures by Age Group, 1977 and 1987." *Health Care Financing Review* 10, no. 4, pp. 116–20.

Ware, J. E., M. S. Bayliss, W. H. Rogers, M. Kosinski, and A. R. Tarlov. 1996. "Differences in 4-Year Health Outcomes for Elderly and Poor, Chronically Ill Patients Treated in HMO and Fee-for-Service Systems." *Journal of the American Medical Association* 276, no. 13, pp. 1039–47.

Ware, J. E., R. H. Brook, W. H. Rogers, E. B. Keeler, A. R. Davies, C. D. Sherbourne, G. A. Goldberg, P. Camp, and J. P. Newhouse. 1986. "Comparison of Health Outcomes at a Health Maintenance Organisation With Those of Fee-for-Service Care." *Lancet,* May 3, pp. 1017–22.

Weiner, S. E. 1993. "New Estimates of the Natural Rate of Unemployment." *Economic Review* (Federal Reserve Bank of Kansas City), fourth quarter, pp. 53–69.

Weinstein, M. M. 1998. "Uttering the P-Word with Social Security." *New York Times,* June 28, sec. 3, p. 1.

Weisbrod, B. A. 1991. "The Health Care Quadrilemma: An Essay on Technological Change, Insurance, Quality of Care, and Cost Containment." *Journal of Economic Literature* 24, no. 2, pp. 523–551.

Weisbrot, M. 1997. *Unequal Sacrifice: The Impact of Changes Proposed by the Advisory Council on Social Security.* Washington, D.C.: Preamble Center.

Wolff, E., and H. Chernick. 1996. *The Distributional Effects of Raising the Retirement Age and Partially Indexing Social Security Benefits.* Washington, D.C.: Economic Policy Institute.

Woolhandler, S., and D. U. Himmelstein. 1998. *For Our Patients, Not for Profits: A Call to Action.* Cambridge, Mass.: The Center for National Health Program Studies.

Woolhandler, S., D. U. Himmelstein, and J. P. Lewontin. 1993. "Administrative Costs in U.S. Hospitals." *New England Journal of Medicine* 329, no. 6, pp. 400–03.

Index

Index